PLAGUE IN SIENA

Studies in Austrian Literature, Culture and Thought

Translation Series

Erich Wolfgang Skwara

PLAGUE IN SIENA

Translated by Michael Roloff,
based on a draft by Derk Wynand

Foreword by Joseph P. Strelka

ARIADNE PRESS

Ariadne Press would like to express its appreciation to the Austrian Cultural Institute, New York and the Austrian Ministry of Education and Art, Vienna, for their assistance in publishing this book.

Translated from *Pest in Siena*, originally published in 1976 by Edition Junge Poesie, Karlsruhe, and in a revised version which forms the basis of this translation by Ullstein Verlag, Berlin, 1983.

Library of Congress Cataloging-in-Publication Data

Skwara, Erich Wolfgang, 1948-
[Pest in Siena. English]
Plague in Siena / Erich Wolfgang Skwara : translated by Michael Roloff, based on a draft by Derk Wynand ; foreword by Joseph P. Strelka.
p. cm. -- (Studies in Austrian literature, culture, and thought. Translation series)
ISBN 0-929497-81-3
I. Title. II. Series.
PT2681.K8P4713 1994
833'.914--dc20 94-4180
CIP

Cover Design:
Art Director, Designer: George McGinnis

270 Goins Court
Riverside, CA 92507

Printed in the United States of America.
ISBN 0-929497-81-3

Foreword

"The weariness of entirely forgotten peoples—I cannot shed it from my eyelids," reads one of the most famous lines of the young Hofmannsthal. But, as compared to that author's apparent youthfulness, the line points to the hidden, heavily graviting treasures of a thousand-year-old cultural inheritance, signals the collected wisdoms of the soul and of historical dependencies that have sunk into the darkest depths of the unconscious psyche.

The basic attitude of the protagonist of *Plague in Siena*, though similar, must be understood differently however: On the one hand, *Plague in Siena* bears strong autobiographical resemblance to its author who was twenty-four at the time he composed this book. Traits of his are merged with those of the centuries-old figure of Don Juan who, in his first literary version by Tirso de Molina, "still maintains a relationship to the Saracens in Moorish Spain, and who had escaped the great *Plague in Siena*" – and the weariness of those forgotten peoples and cultures reverberates in the mind and heart of the autobiographical young protagonist.

But this Don Juan is not just a man of our days in the widest sense of the word, say like Hermann Broch's Herr von Juna who is the archetypal embodiment of the figure of the soul-hunter. The concept of seduction in *Plague in Siena* is meant to be understood in a wider, less direct but symbolic sense. This Don Juan goes far beyond the seduction of women and becomes synonymous with the ambivalent—positively and negatively regarded—old cultural heritage as a whole, which inheritance the seducer confronts as someone who has been seduced! For it is not by chance that we are introduced to Don Juan in Venice, aggregation of cultures that is literally sinking into the water of the Mediterranean, and which here must be regarded as a chiffre, a condensation of European, especially Latin culture as a whole, and of course also of its European microcosmic cultural synthesis, Austria: Venice, after all, belonged for a time to the Habsburg monarchy.

But Skwara's attitude no more than resembles Hofmannsthal's; he only fleetingly imprecates the latter's position, not least because there exist considerable differences in the intellectual make-up of the two youthful authors, but chiefly because Skwara occupies an entirely different position within the system of intellectual coordinates.

Of course, Skwara, too, stands in the tradition of Hofmannsthal who, in a narrow sense of the word, is homeless, surrenders himself to each and every wave just like Skwara's Don Juan. But Hofmannsthal is also someone who lavishly squanders the cultural inheritance—an inheritance, to which, though it may be endangered by death and decline, he nonetheless feels unquestionably bound, so that this cultural body transports him effortlessly, hoveringly as it were, through the abysses and gardens of life. And Hofmannsthal neither sees nor desires a release from these bonds.

The Don Juan of *Plague in Siena*, the "inheritor" of this novel, however represents a different position for its author, for whom this cultural possession no longer embodies an unquestioned positive value, who senses both the positive and negative sides of its seductive character.

It is not by mere chance that Skwara wrote the novel after his first short visit to the United States, after he had been immediately fascinated by the country's size and by the optimism about its future that it exerted then. "Don Juan" traveled to the U.S.A. because of a girl, and after returning to Europe with a curious sense of rebirth, he knew that he was now in a position to let go of this Europe. The painful act of letting go, the backward-looking apotheosis of the Occidental inheritance was caught by the author in the figure of Don Juan, in his centuries-heavy memories of the artistic, literary, humanist, cultural tradition, in his meditations which tend towards the lyrical; and in his observations, yearnings, longing and threshold experiences.

This protagonist, this Don Juan, is a gentleman with demonic features whom apparently everything is forgiven because of his grace, his charm, his sensitivity and education, and whom everything should be forgiven, since he seems superior to a heavy, crude, lowlife way of inflicting injuries. He has the deepest affinities to fin-desiècle culture, to the music of Chopin, to the poetry of Oscar Wilde, and to the despairs of Vincent van Gogh. In other words he is a descendant of the inwardness-obsessed aestheticizing valence of "Viennese modernism" around Hofmannsthal and Bahr. He is a transitional figure, something between dandy and clown, but he is consistently an "always and everything fool" as he calls himself once; someone who is not of the here and now, who is as comical as a circus clown, his transcending sensuality is that of a Pierrot Lunaire, although he is anything but antisensual; and the heathen spirit of his Mediterranean past reverberates through the way he lives.

In short, he is not a realistic hero: and "although he has a driver's license and credit cards and wears ties and modern suits" he is many hundreds of years old. This Don Juan stands in the line of succession of surreal, partially grotesque, in part absurd literary figures of fantastic realism, which reaches from Gütersloh's Count Lunarin to Hahnl's hermits on the Anninger mountain, and Jakov Lind's soul of wood to Peter Marginter's Firbas Goldfuss.

Hovering between pure being and play, learning and sybaritism, perversion and purity of a saint, there arises in this Don Juan a figure to whom "earlier" and "later" are meaningless concepts: always underway—on the road—he nonetheless remains without movement. He is a figure which combines the old Austrian socially determined ability for relativization with that of the new, universal, scientific insights; and thus he runs through the entire gamut of his feelings, his senses, his soul, and nerve sensations, until finally, after the last chapter, "Umbrian Fatigue," he dissolves in the Mediterranean. But this dissolution, too, is not to be understood as a physical death of drowning, nor as an outer or inner act of dying, but as a symbolic act which is related to the author's disappearance—in the sense of his leavetaking from Europe.

Erich Wolfgang Skwara's as it were pre-existential capacity to sense this development did not deceive him: for soon after he wrote this novel he returned to the U.S.A., and today is its citizen. Although here on this continent less than ever before, can he "shed the weariness of entirely forgotten peoples from his eyelids," he is a figure caught in the in-between, at home on two continents, a someone who—with the Austrian gift for compromise, for harmony and for synthesis—seeks to meld the old and the new, which intent of course already points to some of the author's later but, as of this writing, already completed and published works. Yet already in this first novel, the old is, as it were, aired out and cleansed through the perspective of that anti-Faustian Don Juan of whom the author himself declares that he, like his book—though conceived and written in German—has nothing in common with that tradition. Yet the novel's unarticulated inward turn toward the universal is a significant feature of the most extraordinary works of the German intellectual tradition.

The novel appeared in 1976 in a comparatively

small first edition with a courageous small German publisher (Klaus E. R. Lindemann, editor), and though the work scarcely enjoyed a reception at that time, Skwara was writing even more than he is now against the grain of the modish trend.

Despite all their differences, the author Skwara and his hero Don Juan, he and his novel, have as their perhaps most important commonality the gift of a graceful form of communicative interchange. The apple-cheeked poet of *Plague in Siena*, who dined with Henry de Montherlant in Paris, young Skwara who read Dante in the original and befriended the exiled author Hans Sahl in New York, who was infatuated with Trakl as a student in Salzburg, and who while studying in Paris was the friend of world-renowned musicians, has lived as scarcely anyone of his or of any generation has and, inwardly, is most intimately related to his Don Juan in whose distant memories there still stood "the narrow alleys of his childhood in Seville, the paternal Caffè Greco in Rome, and the wretched but majestic citadel of Lisbon, from where he had believed he comprehended Europe."

But this Europe, where he escaped the plague in Siena in 1348, now in the twentieth Century is no longer worthy of the plague. Suddenly a second escape becomes decisive: from a situation which he has reached after a long dream-journey, and which seems to permit of no escape. The freezing yet radiant Don Juan, no longer a guest, finds his escape and a genuinely new beginning—just like his author—in the entrance into music; and just like the poet, he experiences—say in the olive trees that

Van Gogh created in Saint Rémy, in his knowledge of Auschwitz, at the edge of a certain Lake Compounce in Connecticut, where an Indian princess is supposed to have drowned—that the "madness of being able to walk on your own two feet" suddenly makes sense, even if most people in the surroundings of the lake scarcely remember how to get to the water: "in a land where there is a Lake Compounce not everything is lost."

It isn't only these and similar insights, but finally also this which connects me to Erich Wolfgang Skwara whom I did not meet until after I had read his books and had written these words to the German paperback edition. I only knew his voice on the telephone which sounds restless and always on the go as though it did not come from inside him but from his Don Juan. I believe in this author chiefly because he has lived the central human experience of the distrust and fear of death and has perceived it with greater sensitivity and more deeply in the style of his breathless existence than most of us. And because it becomes clear especially from this that his chief concern is scarcely aestheticism, but the lived life.

What concerns him most of all, he said himself in a brief postscript to the first German edition: "Because blindness is not open to me, because I detest irony, I have to find my own way, and that is once and for all. You don't just live in terror of the so-called major events but you live in a continuous good-bye which has been placed inside us in childhood and which to cultivate is our greatest art of surviving. As far as I am concerned: I am panicky by midday at the thought of the coming evening, and not one ought to say to me that tomorrow there begins a new day. All that counts is this, today's day."

Regarded from this as from just about every other perspective, the novel proves to be a variation not on the pure epic, but largely on the lyrical essayistic novel whose fragmentation of form and action is pushed largely into the background, and which lets the author's own, almost entirely indirectly mediated position, appear to be ambivalent. Although obviously without conscious intent in that respect, Skwara renews and continues no less a tradition of the novel than that of Bely, Proust and Rilke.

Joseph P. Strelka
Translation: Michael Roloff

FOR MY DEAD

When
you make dark
in you
stars step out

Draw blood
from the presence
of bodies
untouched

But you
hunt what is falling
you ravish
blazing cheeks

You
a stranger
seek
life and hand

CHAPTER I

He leaned over the edge of the ship. Half attached to something solid, his torso projected near-horizontally above the waves, he surrendered his body to the arbitrariness of the water, to these intimations of sinking. He was on his way, yet remained motionless. He had left his Venice already once too many times to ever be able to truly leave this city for good. As everywhere else, Don Juan was at home here, too, and as everywhere else he was at home nowhere. The ride across the lagoon revealed to him new insights: outlooks really, across the sea, over the beaches, and the skewed view from his near-horizontal position allowed him to perceive the curvature of the earth. Finally he had a presentiment of the patience that water must achieve to become spherical, and he received knowledge of the accumulated tension that inheres in creation, so that it won't shatter.

This his knowledge made Don Juan beautiful, and people were friendly to him, so long as they didn't know his name. It happened that he met young women when he sensed how easy it would be to resume his old arts of seduction. But then he recalled how people, especially women, were invariably far too young, and this realization pained him, and he let the beautiful beings pass, and he sighed. He knew that all other peoples' talents for surrender and for the arts of love was as nothing but a game in his life, a heavy breathing was all they were while he himself would have wanted nothing more, finally, than to be vulnerable through closeness to one other. An ambition to grow smaller seized him. But he had never mastered surrender, which is why he did not have to die.

Calculating, we know only inexactly how old Don Juan actually is, or would be today, but dependable sources tell us that he was one of the few who survived the great plague in Siena, and we know that he had been on friendly terms with the Saracens of Moorish Spain. Historical events encompass Don Juan like the bars of a cage, speak a language all their own.

Don Juan met people, but he didn't need encounters. What he needed was the one encounter, a certainty of loving, but the satisfaction of this particular hunger was his worst failure. He learned to realize that in all the centuries he hadn't obtained the slightest knowledge of the human soul. No worse psychologist existed than Don Juan. He had certainly acquired a rough understanding of his victims, but he didn't know human beings. They remained as unpredictable for him as for all of us.

* * *

Yes, he had really grown old. He had finally gotten through the trashy parts of his life that are rife in the literature about him, and nothing remained of that, nay, but a trace of nausea and of a yearning for purity. He consoled himself in the thought that true innocence did not belong to childhood, but that it had to be won in life, and he continued to flirt mildly with this notion. At the same time Don Juan mistrusted his convictions, and now that he was aging he was certain of only one thing, namely that he had led a chaste life. He could not of course deny that he had seduced one thousand and three women and girls in Spain alone, but in the new and better account Don Juan was preparing, the many female bodies became cold cloister walls. His former extravagance had been a form of chastity somewhat hard to understand. Only now did Don Juan yearn for his first love in order to escape his solitude.

He knew that he had to hurry, and that this love, which still needed to be found, might yet lend his life the meaning it had so far lacked. He also wanted to meet love's conditions, wanted to be shy, awkward and anxious: in short, to be a different man from the one he had been. But above all, he finally wanted to learn how to weep, not just to see other people's tears. Don Juan wondered about so-called happiness. Yet until he had reached the point of craving these simple values, so much time had passed that now Don Juan was living amongst us, in this century. Like the rest of us, he was obliged to take part at least in the superficies of this world. He had a driver's license and various credit cards, and he wore suits and ties of course. Yet he lived off to the side, only seldom getting it right.

Many scholarly and, what is worse, creative works had been written about him. Indeed, Don Juan had always had to put up with fabrications purporting to know and see through him, but in the last hundred years the flood gates had opened. More and more unsolicited authors, whom Don Juan did not even know personally, appeared. Formerly, at least, men of some stature had had it out with him, which was some consolation. Though of course even these had too often overlooked what was crucial, it was nevertheless flattering, despite all misunderstanding, to be misapprehended by a Herr Wolfgang Mozart, to be damned rather unjustly within the most daring work of genius. You might accept being consigned to hell by Signor da Ponte, but to be banished to hell by music too was sometimes painful. Yet all these minor irritations were negated by the aura of being a famous European. Should we say: having been? For much had changed in the meantime. Whoever wrote about Don Juan these days reduced him to a case study.

For all that, Don Juan was healthy, or restored to health at least. His disposition had always been internationalist, and when Europe was still divided into a thousand principalities and kingdoms, he felt at home in all of them. His life, apparently confused, but in fact mathematically ordered, had for centuries borne the seal of great Europeanism and humanism. And these were the two concepts Don Juan liked to whisper to himself as he walked through the rows of trees: Europeanism, humanism. But the sound of these words drained him of hope. Precisely for that reason, being universally famous had a curative effect. Applause only too frequently is a distraction for those who are unhappy or depressed—from the ominous clouds. But fame has its darker side: everyone, almost everyone misunderstood Don Juan, and for no good reason he had far too quickly become an allegory for no end of womanizing lowlife. As though it didn't matter who does the seducing, who pulls the strings. Don Juan had little use for symbolism, since he was practically immortal.

Because hardly anyone knows it, it should here be mentioned that for centuries Don Juan had tried to write an autobiography. He did not want to do so out of vanity, but to put an end to these unsolicited people's turning his life into the titles of their books. But however often he had begun to write, the first lines went stale under his hand. He was a virtuoso at pleasuring alien bodies, but for that reason alone, because he knew about lust and joy, his hands shied away from the tedium of writing. Second-hand living was nothing for Don Juan. Yet he would gladly have seen his affairs set aright, would gladly have put the precise memory of his life into impartial hands. But impartial hands are not an artist's hands, nor a scholar's hands, and certainly not the hands of love. Don Juan knew this, but he was unwilling to draw the consequences of his self-denial so long as he was waiting for the admittedly quite improbable eventuality of his becoming a human being. It was a question of one word that could convince him. But he was of course hard to please, for, as we know, he was an aging man.

* * *

The day was not over by far, and yet it was already filled with great experiences. Even in the morning, when Don Juan had been drinking tea on the piazza, in the Caffè Florian as always, in the salon with the nubile Rococo lamps, and when, on the pretext of a completed hour, all the city bells had suddenly begun to toll, he sensed an important day in the offing. Within the sound of these bells, streaming in from all sides, even discord became harmony. The city's former greatness, which Don Juan had experienced and which had stayed in his mind like an image of the Holy Grail, seemed preserved, for this century, solely within the bells of the island churches and in the possibility of their tolling. From the vibrations pealing across the lagoon a good spirit issued, a gentle breeze that promised the people and their ships a fortunate journey.

In that hour, Don Juan had cast aside all memories, the orgastic as well as the sublime. He was finally free and conscious of what he amounted to. The city of Venice, which he had assumed he had exhausted, still held everything in store for him: now, after its fairy tales, its reality.

Aboard the ship, he cultivated his artificial nausea and as he watched the sliced foaming green water sliding by like swarms of fish in its disappearance act in back, he day-dreamed lucidly about the major pact, the compromise, that would be concluded here, silently and yet quite publicly. The hard and the soft yielded to each other, both relinquishing their soul a little, and the result was this gliding that allowed the spirit to lie down horizontally with a body and to play. It was something to be sure, oh yes, and taking courage now, Don Juan wondered whether all events in and beyond the world did not depend an a balancing of hardness, and whether the requirement for creation was not mildness, speaking more softly, making more fluid, in short: mitigation.

When he leaned over the ship's railing, he could enjoy the gliding and the cool wind as a form of delicious nourishment. What, he thought, if the ship runs aground on a sandbank? The quiet day will end horribly, people will scream and go down screaming, broken parts will float off unfeeling. The wind will no longer caress the gentle people; it will no longer spoil our hair—the death of one human being and all human beings actually cease to exist.

Most of all Don Juan feared what was swift. The gentle forging ahead of yourself which tended to shift, at the flick of the wrist, into something treacherous, the seductive acceleration, could lose itself and its own form before it found time to take leave. Dying was not so bad, if only it allowed for a leave-taking. An airplane and a human face were subject to the same laws, and were beautiful so long as they remained themselves. So long as there was a gentle gliding, the world too was saved. But the increase in acts of extreme violence was nearly exponential, and this exhausted Don Juan, even if he only read these facts in the papers. What was gentle seemed to be vanishing and this uncanny disappearance was a threat to Don Juan's existence. He was determined to continue, to go on living, so long as the water remained soft and allowed for sinking.

Formerly he had found compensation for hardness in the soft bodies of women, later more so in music, but now Don Juan came to understand that the softness that mattered was unconditional. The angular, jagged world was soft above all. Actually softness was easier to discover in the world's hollows and bumps than on its beaten paths. Therefore Don Juan no longer absorbed himself exclusively in the arts and in music, but also in the confusion of the cities, statistics, and common people. Suddenly he found a gliding everywhere, and he knew that the conditions for harmony expand as we broaden ourselves. He no longer loved youth in order to sleep with it, but for that softness missing at its heart, and because all that mattered was that its gentle lines sank deeper, burrowed in, trickling through life into life.

When the ship glided past a dead dog floating in the water, Don Juan did not find the animal ugly in the least. The spongy cadaver proved that what was hard was patiently growing softer here, and what evidence for this experience could be more conclusive than death? So the passengers finally reached the shore, where the captain docked routinely and gently. On the land again, the images entered Don Juan that much more deeply.

* * *

He met the girl and spoke with her. A few phrases, a few beginnings, allusions to the summer festival.

The girl had invited guests to the summer festival who knew the extent of mourning in which the gardens lie embedded. The girl had not planned the summer festival; rather she had raised it as others raise children, with all possible care, with all possible love. When the summer festival finally took place, rolled across the garden stage, the laughter was too loud and too obvious. The girl had to admit that some guests were not grieved: these joyous people became an embarrassment.

Don Juan could be happy he had not shown up at the summer festival—a shabby joy of thoughtlessness that had set the flowers on fire. Until this day it remained undetermined who all had died at this summer festival. Nothing but ashes had remained on the following morning, and no one knew who was in the ashes. Nor was it possible to look for survivors, for, when the flames leapt highest, the crowd had scattered. The summer festival had become the darkest of dark nights, said the girl with an inflectionless voice.

But Don Juan felt he had kindlier thoughts about the summer festival than she, the girl, did, and that he had indeed been there that night. He had worn his silk suit and he had seen how joy had set the flowers ablaze. It had been the flowers' fault, not joy's crime. For a long time now the flowers had refused the rain of delight, for which reason alone they blazed as they did. She, the girl, should be happy about the summer festival. It had been a grand success, also for the dead. But the girl wept and did not believe a word he said.

Don Juan was glad to see the lovely hostess again. She had been too busy during the festival to find time to talk. They had noticed each other so fleetingly the young girl had already forgotten the old man. But this kind of forgetfulness is not as easily accomplished in reverse for the superannuated.So it was a pleasure today to have the opportunity to go for a walk.

* * *

—I'm not surprised we knew each other fleetingly. All of us know one another fleetingly. When I walk around the lake, for instance, I wonder whether there's anyone I know better than you, my girl, my so fleeting acquaintance. I also think of the summer festival when I walk around the lake. And since I keep getting older, the lake's circumference seems greater and greater, whereas my life seems more and more confined. The curves extend themselves into straightaways. No one knows my lake, Lake Compounce, and it will have dried up before it is known.

—I went swimming in Lake Compounce. I ignored the warning about snakes. I swam out to the middle of the lake and reached for the shore at a different slant. Whenever I stepped ashore I found the tracks of a narrow-gauge railway, and the large forest behind. Whoever wants to find Lake Compounce needs eyes and good maps. But I am familiar with the lake and I imagine I know it better even than my hometown Seville. In fact, Lake Compounce is my lake.

—Why do I even bring up the lake? Because it is so horribly irrelevant and because I want to hold on to it, because it deserves of importance. Unfortunately, Maria Obolensky, the love I neglected, didn't know this lake. She would certainly have come to like it. Yet sometimes I am afraid of becoming tangled in the crazy thought that Maria Obolensky would have taken neither me nor the lake into her life. She contained everything and, self-sufficiently, needed no one. But Lake Compounce needed me. People have always refused to drive to the lake with me. Most of them called it boring but some gave their real reason. They thought Lake Compounce was dangerous. They knew that its waters saddened me. In fact, the lake shore was intimately related to the death that I did not die. Lake Compounce was I, was one with me. Now, that I have long lost my former self, am no longer identical with it, have nearly forgotten it, only the lake continues to be me. It has a peculiarly mirroring surface that preserves what is lost. No one unprepared to accept eternity should lean over Lake Compounce.

—I admit that I've talked only rarely about the land on the other side, my real homeland and I'll go on keeping that *beyond* to myself. I'll keep silent. True, it is an annoyance that public opinion insists on making me a Spaniard to this very day, even though I suffered only a small share of my lust in that part of Europe. For me, Spain, that wretched and proud country, is nothing but my dusty childhood, the castle I lost centuries ago. Of course, they still point out my tavern in Seville, but couldn't every tavern in the world be mine? I've been a guest everywhere.

—The roads avoid Lake Compounce, of course, and whoever wants to reach down to its shores must first look for the approach. A sharp curve to the left that even practiced drivers keep taking too fast. The tires squeal then and the gravel sprays up. Taking that private road is of course interdicted, and most cars turn back at the sign. It takes a bit of nerve, it takes a bit of courage to reach the lake.

—Then the path ends in an amusement park. Behind the sheds a Ferris wheel rises steeply into the air. The ghost-ride has been padlocked. The restaurant is made entirely of clapboard that hungrily awaits that lightning strike. The lake extends behind that. Its waves exist as a suggestion; their slapping manifests no enthusiasm. No major holidays are celebrated here anymore, but festive possibilities are inherent in the place. A few keys should suffice to unlock the sheds. A few burning torches to chase out rats and spiders and a few buckets of fresh paint to rekindle a world of wonders should suffice. The marvelous holiday ought to overshadow the lake's beauty. But Lake Compounce lies in a shadow; the mountains are too close, too high. The sun begins to fade away into the forest by three o'clock in the afternoon.

—Indians used to live there a long time ago. The saying is that their princess drowned in the lake. The people around the lake know this story, but scarcely know the approach to the water.

—Destitute newcomer that I was, I of course had no car to take me to Lake Compounce and so I began to walk the roads, for hours, always by myself. In America footsteps lead to nothing. Drivers stared at me, dogs raged after me. There are neither fences nor borders in America, everyone lives at the mercy of whoever happens by. After I'd walked for hours, the low-lying sun forced me to stop. I looked around; I was still at the same spot. Yet I had to go back, make my way back, back through the darkness for hours. When I finally reached my bed, I cried myself to sleep.

—I would have liked to have met the princess. I loved the calm lake as her double, her larger body. Sleeping alone is an agony when you hear the clock ticking. But most human beings are dumb and blind, a world ignorant of the curse of missing the boat.

—When I first glimpsed the lake, I finally knew my place in the new land. That September was torrid and Lake Compounce did me good. The madness of going on foot began to make sense on the lake shore. In a country where Lake Compounce exists, all is not lost. But whoever fails to find the lake will certainly go insane in a world where walking must remain futile. The lake had saved my life. I could walk only along the tracks, elsewhere there was no room because of the forest. The train on its narrow tracks must have delighted the children once. One round might have cost a quarter, and it was worth it, it was worth it.

* * *

—Behind the train, the mountains rise, erratic, rocky, and behind these the weekend hunters level their rifles at wild ducks. You flinch at every shot. But today this lake has played out its most important role. I owe an enduring gratitude to it. Walking, I'd completed the round time and again, ending at the Ferris wheel, my starting point. My steps, despite the forbidding continent, had become steps again. Each rounding of the lake corresponded to a feeling, and every arrival brought to me a solitary joy. Until I finally made out the car that came to take me back to the others, who called my circumambulations madness, who never understood my arrivals.

—When the muteness of encounters remained like blue smoke on the roads, I, the habitué of coldness, would think about *her*. There's no evidence for her death, as there's no evidence for her having lived. Words fail and mathematical formulae fail. A diagram of her life lacks the green of the most widespread trees. Perhaps he who places flowers on her marbled arm is infringing on the rights of a closer acquaintance. So Maria Obolensky lives on, and she has not wept for many years. "She and I and what we are missing: pardon this *we*, my love."

—Perhaps there is nothing wrong with this story except for my remembering and telling it. The articulation must be the mistake. Yet I don't want to remember anything, not a thing, and especially not this story. I want to spare myself and my subject, though I am not the problem here, and even less of a problem is the callowness of "sparing."

—Because less and less becomes sayable, because hardly a word can survive, speech grows poorer and yet the wealth of our silence sees no surfeit. Again, we seek ways to reach Maria Obolensky and we seek the honor of calling ourselves her friend. But brown pine cones keep plopping from the cypress trees, fall down and explode. A sharp sound, impossible to pinpoint, and already nothing is left us.

—There used to be painters, once there were poets. A few used to compose music, others used to think. We learn these accusations at length in our schools, and the cemetery proves the theses. There used to be men who dined on the terrace in the evening, and the wind would cool their brows. The terraces were built of marble and the gardens were lovely. We heard this thousandfold at school and we believed it. The scent of the flowers was acknowledged then, nor was love always denied. Subject for study, examination jitters.

—Maria Obolensky believed in words, which made her eyes widen and her lips soften. Whether she kissed well we do not know. She may not have been technically adept at love. After all, she died at eighteen, but she certainly had a pronounced talent for tenderness. Her softness accommodated itself to this Rome where she died. Even in those days, being born in Russia and dying in Rome at age eighteen would earn you a favorable notice in the papers.

—The small emptiness that her dying cut into

us—it lasted forever, yet was soon filled. We can safely assume that the sculpture depicting the girl, this legitimate work of art had the kindred effect of a tooth-filling on the survivors' grief: pain-soothing and quick. But we can also assume that no one really knew the girl. People like her just aren't known. Perhaps her life was meaningless, but perhaps it was of utmost importance. Thus it was possible to argue about Maria Obolensky. But who would help her by arguing about her? And ultimately, to argue about her you had to love her. But who could love her since no one knows her? Who knows Maria Obolensky? Just who knows her?

—It would take a sister who had no idea of her sisterhood to find her grave. Only where silence reigns can there be the sudden lightning flash that sets things ablaze. Even the lightning strives to be reflected in language. Wherever a sister lives, a family line is not yet dead, you would suppose. But the flowers around Maria Obolensky are fading, and the sculpture's marble fades. The question about the correct point of time fades in the face of time itself.

—If I, Don Juan, live longer than all of you; if, using certain minor concepts, I can be regarded as immortal, then it's only because I've wasted my life and because dissipation is eternal. You have to undertake what's senseless and evil to be sure of duration. But now that I'm talking about failed love, about Maria Obolensky, I already feel my age, my very proximate death. You merely need to think about what is serious and you begin to die.

How seriously, talking about seriousness. . . . I think about this girl again. She died because she was prepared to brave love (her face betrays this preparedness). I am alive because I am incapable of surrender. If my guilt in having come too late did not lie between us, your grave would be without flowers now.

—Maria Obolensky, this forbidden thought, this singular name, is repeatedly uttered behind the wall that separates her grave from the noisy road. A few more years and the wall too will be torn down. Aren't they building this world just so they can tear it down? Razing cemeteries is simple, simpler than annihilating a city. When the living, who are ill-bred, begin to cry inarticulately, the dead will of course remain mute. Even Maria Obolensky, who has much to say, would remain silent if someone snatched her grave. That's the one major advantage the dead have, and the most important difference between them and us: they do not bemoan trifles.

—At her grave a sound can sometimes be heard. It does not ask to be pronounced, it is imprecise and resembles the sighs of lovers. And of course is the humming of the dead, who are nestling into and surrendering themselves to this earth that is theirs. It accepts us tenderly, unconditionally because we make no difference to it. Extraordinary: the humming of the dead.

—Where Vincent the painter (another friend whom I failed), whereas this Vincent had the strength to despair of a few stars and a few cypress trees, Maria Obolensky can only summon

the weakness to lack all motion and yearning. But death has nothing to do with weakness.
—Vincent's world did not suddenly turn dark, his mind did not become part of the night then, but is becoming so in the here and now where it seeks for shade beneath the unbearable stars, whereas Maria Obolensky only died away then. Pathetic victims of their rotting aristocratic lungs, those who were consigned to death became ethereally beautiful and their ending resounded like chamber music. Maria Obolensky's dying scarcely bothered with the make-up of despair. If we weep no tears for her, today, it is only because our grief exceeds her absence. Our grief has become greater . . . some words know no bounds and soon there'll be no mouth that calls after the dead.
—The aging grandee dreams that Maria Obolensky is his lover. The girl remains loyal to us. Plastic flowers still blossom in front of her grave. This lapse in taste is a good sign.
—And don't be afraid of the *thou*! Certainly, I won't become tasteless and weep; I certainly won't become self-important. At most we'll stroke your stone-rendered hair, though our lives and our moments of tenderness are too impatient and brief to threaten your marble. For though we know that each caress transforms a small part of marble to dust and steals it away, the sum of these stolen goods fails to increase quickly enough to endanger your hair. Thieves are harmless, Maria Obolensky; only the uncaring are dangerous, those who don't love you, who let the dust gather on you.
—But I see that I've hopelessly given myself up to

these faithless words that betray me. Because we cannot weep, because we cannot love, we want to speak and find the words that will justify what makes us fall silent. On the street I notice the people becoming more beautiful, that my body longs for them, but that all relationships with people are becoming uglier and more absurd. I long for their bodies, but if I possessed them, I wouldn't know what to do. I've had many people, some only after a long siege; they were lovely victories for me, but in memory they carry no weight. I, Don Juan, have no memories, and as for Maria Obolensky, I've failed with her and everything else.

CHAPTER II

The attendants blithely unaware, he sat whole afternoons on the green painted bench in the park of the enclosed sanatorium rehearsing his return to the so-called world. He imagined that he had had a face lift in the hospital, that he had discarded his name and his controversial reputation once and for all, that he was no longer Don Juan. He looked younger now, but also more mortal. Yet he could not complain about these traces of his mortality, for he had entered the sanatorium of his own accord. He had driven his identity as Don Juan to an intolerable pitch; now he wanted to make a fresh start, wanted to stop being himself. He had been preparing this transformation a long time. He kept it a secret from others, of course, and concealed it so well from himself that he finally forgot about it. He became accustomed to the institution. Not until the end of summer did he recall the true reason for his stay in the *maison de santé*, did he become conscious of his painstakingly acquired mortality. In long whispered monologues in the park, he rationalized that he had reached the very limits of medicine and the thinking that lay behind it—the doctors, these backdrops, could do nothing further for him. He was healthy, had always been healthy in fact and had no idea he was registered as a permanent guest in the sanatorium's files. The doctors deemed him incurable; the patient deemed himself healthy.

He loved this hospital, and he loved it all the more because he intended to stay only a few days longer. He loved the large garden especially, and toward evening, when the maple trees emphatically grew blacker, he would sometimes cling fearfully to the wooden bench. He had rearranged his life and made a new beginning, but he could not rid himself of a few habits that were dear or necessary to him. Thus he hated the darkness, feared clouds and longed for death when the wood of the garden benches grew damp at night. Tears made him both sad and furious, for he did not care to admit that every being and everything could weep. Endlessly he had trailed dry-eyed through the lovely park, and the few islands in his life—especially sunken islands—where he had wept, bore remote, forgotten names. During his walks through the garden's scented beauty, he carefully avoided the high walls that separated the sanatorium from the other world. Yet the insurmountable walls were not an insurmountable obstacle for him. Though he was considered incurable, the doctors thought him a harmless case who had the right to come and go as he liked. He could have gone out twice a week, should have gone out for therapeutic reasons, but he did not want to. He rather re-arranged endlessly the contents of his suitcase, which were familiar to him even in his sleep and yet which fascinated him time and again. Why did he prefer to stay in his room? Besides, the danger that the patient could run amok at the next crossroad or be run over inadvertently was no greater for him than for all of us.

He was transformed yet did not trust his metamorphosis. "If I go out," he feared, "someone might recognize me. Someone might shout, there goes Don Juan, and that would be the end of my life as another man. First I must be sure that my transformation has been a success." Certainly he did not tell the doctors about these reflections. Rather he chatted about the garden's charm without sounding all too convincing. It was assumed that he had the first symptoms of the so-called institutional syndrome, which, after too long a stay, renders the patient's outside environment alien, can disenable him for life. How wrong these good doctors were in his case! If anything, the patient had achieved his ultimate freedom in this hospital and only here had acquired the capacity to leave the sanatorium and live outside it. Actually he wanted to be gone already. He should not be sitting in the garden admiring nature's beauty. But he already felt again the terrible bonds he had never felt for human beings but only for places and exigencies. He should have noticed that he was putting himself in danger. In these sultry afternoons, he could already have been called Don Juan again, and that was the dangerous threshold where the cure became poison. Now his departure had become really urgent.

* * *

He still spent his days in the park. He realized

that he had no destination. He began to consider specific details of the journey he could hardly postpone any longer, the numerous little stage directions he had to set himself, for as of this moment he would be actor and director in one, as is the fashion. He also had to dismiss several doubts, had to approach a few of the dead within him and distance himself from a few other dead, and had to pack his suitcase yet and lock it for all time to come. This locking became the most important item of his departure; his life would stand or fall with the closed suitcase lock. For it only made sense to have a suitcase if you were never to open it again. Possessing a suitcase is justified only if its contents are familiar to the owner; otherwise the case will turn into a nightmare. A further difficulty was the first decision that had to be made: in which hand should he carry the suitcase? Which hand, left or right, was more suitable; which could be called steadier? That alternating was out of the question was clear from the outset. If he carried the case of his past in his right hand, then he would be forever excused. But if he carried it in his left hand, there would be freedom, to be sure, but no credible pretext to avoid unwanted encounters. Whoever welcomes the future without reservations is of course most vulnerable. He had to decide very conscientiously which policy to adopt that of the handshake or that of being incapacitated.

Now even the doctors insisted on urging him to step out on his two days of freedom. They instilled courage in him, using their felonious method of suggesting ever new hope. Don Juan did not need their help; he was overflowing with hope. He even managed to convince his attendants that the leaves were already bright and autumnal, that death already lay dormant in the garden, whereas the world was still a voluptuous green. His neighbors, the real patients, moved sluggishly through the lovely park, and many of them greeted the potential escapee. They even greeted him with studied politeness as they slouched past him. One came along and absently said: "If I keep going in a straight line, I'll reach my destination!"

The sentence was spoken wearily, its substance surely the *sum* of years of disease. Although the man of the world needed no encouragement, the words filled Don Juan, who thought himself transformed, with tremendous strength and terrible wanderlust. Briefly he recalled the narrow alleys of his Seville childhood, the paternal Caffè Greco in Rome, and the wretched but majestic citadel of Lisbon, whence he thought he had understood Europe across the Rio Tejo on clear nights. He remained lost in these snowballing memories for a while, then rushed back to the sanatorium and packed his suitcase. He placed books on the bottom, wrapped manuscripts and letters in old newspapers, and embedded the few engravings and etchings he still owned in silk shirts.

As he walked through the park for the last time—meanwhile it had grown dark—he felt something like guilt. He would go now, simply run away, after the state—he did not know which, but there was a state everywhere—had paid for his stay here. He did not like others to pay for him, but there was no other possibility, since he had no new wealth and knew no people, so that personal help was out of the question. Should he now, say out of gratitude, end his life in this sanatorium? Perhaps it was shabby and would cause vile gossip to let the state pay his keep and then to depart secretly, but unfortunately there was no other choice. He already saw the wall's shadow. In any case the small act of ingratitude he was about to commit struck him as more human and excusable than the prolonged, ongoing guilt of staying put. He should have no scruples now; it was not the state that had paid for him, but only he and he alone who bore the costs of his life. It was fair enough that people like him should not take public handouts, since they should not take any handouts whatsoever, since they could not grasp any hand and remain true to themselves. These were his thoughts as he whisked past the sleeping watchman to the outside.

* * *

Walking tired him. He had not counted on becoming tired. During his past life he had only walked on lawns and paced the parquet floor of his castles, and now that he set foot an asphalt, each yard was agony. He was too tired to think, but in fact he should have thought about the kind of fatigue it was that he had to overcome. Not every tiredness is cured by sleeping. Perhaps it was merely this unaccustomed pavement that was exhausting the man who had come from the institution. Or perhaps it was his stolen freedom that was tiring him. Incidentally, he was carrying his suitcase in his left hand, which kept him free for encounters. But now it was too late, and the terribly empty streets yawned before him, so that he did not need his right hand. The suitcase began to distract its owner: it weighed almost nothing, this suitcase; it had become light as a toy, although it was stuffed full of Don Juan's past. This terrible weightlessness, which would have gladdened any other traveler, transformed the suitcase for Don Juan, or rather, for the man who had once been Don Juan, into a problem case, into a leather monster from which issued the fear that something may have been forgotten in packing it. But here on the open road, he would not and could not check whether his fear had any foundation. Checking would have meant opening it and that was no longer allowed.

As he walked, he calmed down. His horrified questions—did I pack this, did I pack that? And didn't I forget that?—fell asleep. Don Juan began to rejoice in the fact that things and memories simply have less weight than we tend to assume.

* * *

He went on, crossing the midnight border into a new day. But the new day's darkness was alarmingly like the old day's darkness, and it became increasingly difficult to believe that days allegedly end and begin at midnight. Why did the break not take place at noon, when it is bright and when the border might be visible? Certainly these were foolish thoughts, for aren't days the invention of man, the offspring of our lack of imagination,and each such thought, so brooded the walker, diminishes our strength for walking. Better not to think of them at all for the sake of conserving energy for walking on blindly: for life. Travelers ought not to think, was one of his thoughts.

Finally it was daybreak. The new Don Juan was dead tired and, above all, lost in the unfamiliar landscape he had reached. He began to worry that he might have left the sanatorium too early, that he should have rehearsed his journey more thoroughly. The trees and harvested wheat fields that stretched out all around him substituted for the critical audience that he feared. At some time they had all paid for their tickets and now they were expecting a performance for which he was not prepared. Nor could he improvise cleverly, for he was really too tired and besides, it was not in his line; it was not in his line *anymore*. It was terrible to be in no position to perform on the stage of the road and to be at the mercy of the waxing day.

Because he felt helpless and unhappy, he immediately became Don Juan again. He had always been helpless, not demonic, not superior. Only those who are helpless play at being the seducer, so as to cling: victims are powerful. He had been at the sanatorium for nothing; he could not escape his fate. He hated his life and his immortality, but nothing bestows a greater sense of duration than misery. The landscape around him lacked reality, and yet it was more real than anything he had seen before. The trees seemed to be burning, Don

Juan touched his eyes, and the sky loomed overhead, unbearably silent and blue. It was a sunny November day, a last summons to die and sleep, which Don Juan could not heed. He wanted to live yet was overcome by pernicious hope; he did not know how to orient himself hereabouts. Above all, there were no people but only the eager audience, and the silent birds drawing their heavy, inky wings across the spaceless stage.

CHAPTER III

Rushing diagonally over the fields, silent as a wing-beat, there approached a ruddy man who looked like no one in particular yet more ugly than pleasant; and though exhausted and breathless from hurrying, he began to speak at once.

—Wherever we turn: boundaries, increasing bitterness. But something inside us won't be deceived, won't be killed, and hence wherever we turn: sweetly flowing life, radiance everywhere, we take it in and miss it for all that. I didn't get around to painting my truest pictures. Standing on the main square in Ghent, streaking through the fields in Provence are passing states, there is no lasting state. The grief killing us is a passing state, and consider this: discotheques, that easy music, that most extreme form of grief the seems so popular and contemporary, is only a passing folly. People are looking for markings: painting.

Disguised, Don Juan was unsure whether he had really fled the closed sanatorium or not. What this man in front of him said, or rather, what this man poured forth, could no doubt be called correct, but nevertheless or for that very reason—remained hospital speech, institutional jargon.

—And we're in the middle of my craft, of the little lines I've drawn on canvas paper which have become energized without any of my doing. All of us must realize that it's a matter of describing unbearable circumstances, of natural riddles, whose enumeration is the only thing left for us to do. To find their answer: never. You assume I don't know you, but you're wrong, Don Juan, for I know you very well. Not only did the mistral fall down upon both of us in the south, that wind which the winegrowers love as they fear it, but we also heard the same stories: Spanish, Moorish, desert tales, and among all these the one story that concerns you, you, good sir, the story about the small tavern with the dark walnut benches. You look at me, you stare with astonishment, but you shouldn't be astonished, since I've already confessed that I failed to paint my truest pictures, just as you failed. Yes, I'm a painter, and I often use this little word YES, which makes you flinch, you eternal nay-sayer, flinch time and again . . . I employ this little word, yes, at the beginning, in the middle, at the end of sentences, for I forfeited the right to a no long ago, in those days not too far from Paris, in Auvers-sur-Oise. It was quite a valid no, a long-term contract, much too long for an artist in any case. An artist—and aren't we both artists, good sir?—shouldn't draw contracts. But what's done is done, we imagine we ought to be faithful and so we're standing face to face here, you and I, we have succeeded in leaving the night of the fugitives for the day of the damned. My pictures hang in The Hague, hang in Arnhem, are scattered all over, yet my most beautiful pictures are hoarded in Amsterdam. I've been widely shown for some time. Basically, Don Juan, you too are a painter. You only think you're better than that, and you tense your neck muscles for a reply. Save your reply, good sir, and believe me: you too are a painter. I've seen the faces twisted with joy, and the souls twisted with pain, which bore your insignias. Though your fame, Don Juan, is unmatched, you know little about it; you are unaware of the consequences of your life. Maybe that explains your purity.

The one who spoke, spoke wildly, but the style of his speech led Don Juan to believe that he was conversing with a man of his own stature. So he listened out of politeness. With the silence of a Spanish grandee, the thin smile of those drenched with lust, and the candid gaze of a knight of the Grail, he listened to the stranger's words.

—Lighthouses bother me, this myth of their light. Lighthouses, you know, still cast their light when we, you or I, walk through city streets or when we've long lost sight of the shore. Everywhere there are people, everywhere is the world. Can you bear that idea? Lighthouses are said to have something to do with life saving. Here credulousness sets in once more, which has been a problem for me all my life, especially so during the days when I still played at preaching. The headache that the blowing grass gives me, this gentle dancing that weighs more than cast iron certainty. Lets take the certainty of God or merely the certainty of our brush strokes, neither counts, nor anything else, once we are in the dunes and freeze in the wind. Today everyone, in his own fashion, can afford to watch the setting sun emit its last mimicry of itself, watch it either as a fan, as a poet, whatever, because we're backed up by computers which we absolutely refuse to believe in while we make them our absolute masters.

The two strangers began to feel at ease with each other. The morning had advanced; the sun maintained its course toward the zenith.—Sheet-lightning, good sir, wading through life, sending the soul to a spa, lightning-quick immigration. You or I, so long as we're dead—and it's a kind of bond —will have to say no to darkness, as long as we live. Say no to it and to the clouds, these monstrous perversions on the pale horizon . . . I wonder whether stars and self-liberation aren't one and the same, self-liberation being the somewhat more ordinary death. But this question leads to the empty chair with a candle that's burning in Amsterdam now.

—When Paul left me, going away from Arles, going back into his despair, because my own didn't have room for two, an empty chair remained behind, an empty chair and a great deal of night. But chairs hate being empty; they cry out for people to sit on them and grow older on them. That's why Paul left a candle behind, and a book as well: two signs of a solitude even greater than mine was and is no longer . . . The candle was threatened by too much icy pain: My ear! Thus I had to paint the candle and the book too, and the chair . . . and so saved the candle from being blown out. Now the candle glows, and its light lit my way to Auvers-sur-Oise, that flickering point which taught me how to say no and avoid empty chairs from then on. But, good sir, though it seems easy to say now, it's not. What's terrible after a long journey is the inevitable arrival in some room, having to set foot in the hostel or the destination, and this moment frightens us so much that we secretly hope for an accident, some tragedy that will avert the arrival.

* * *

—I too, the renowned fugitive answered, know what it is to listen for the tragedy, know what it is to wait for some fatal disease. When I was staying at the sanatorium from which I just departed, to hurry toward our chance encounter, I saw faces, saw evenings looming, quivering with tension. I should have observed them and fixed their form, but I thought there was still time. Repeatedly I began to write, but I stopped just as often. Now, after my terrible night walk, I'm tired. Wherever I turn—you see, caballero,—your speech has become my speech; your paintings are embellished by the frame of my past—wherever I turn, I see fields, I see plains, I see perfection a thousand fold, but I see no possibilities for a beginner. In the suitcase I'm carrying, there are manuscripts certainly, successful beginnings, the torsos of thoughts, but now that everything's at hand: will, thought, reader and light—my work is missing its base; I can't find a desk anywhere.

* * *

So they talked to each other in riddles, taking a turn they did not choose, that they did not recognize. They listened to each other more attentively now, yet knew that in the final analysis they were speaking nonsense, that their journey and their words were leading them further and further into abstruse and improprietous subjects. But you are not called Don Juan and Vincent with impunity: the judgment carried out against these names was their grotesque passage not only through various countries, but through the centuries. The encounter between the two was not an encounter at all, since personalities such as they were incapable of an encounter.

—Wherever you begin, it's a bad beginning. Spare me my "my-story," my life, which—unlike my pictures—doesn't even consist of brush strokes. There are only brush strokes; even my ravens above the field are two black strokes. The betrayal of art. Strokes too were the calm days in Saint Rémy, that endless silence interrupted only by laughter.

Now the two men reached a tree, a solitary tree in the fields. Vincent asked for indulgence for his incoherent words, which he thought of as offspring of his illness. He was thirsty, he remarked, and he wanted to drink the blue sky. But Don Juan, who was a man of the world, preferred champagne. They thirsted and neither of them received what he sought.

—Absorbed in moss and ferns and sky, we lie stretched out here. We have a yearning that's expressed in patches of speech, mostly we whisper, inaudibly: names, coffee in summer cups, love, Gulbenkian Foundation, Reginald Turner, simplicity . . . We see moths flutter around candles, and we fear for our dirty brushes that suffer from mange and are nearly bare. If we contemplate the creation of afternoons too closely, Mozart's music strikes us like death. Whoever looks up into the tree-tops won't believe in the blossoms, for we don't believe in what's real. I've painted both, good sir: landscapes that are good and exude peace, and landscapes that become so knotted they kill us. They're moods, it's said, humors, but ultimately the two of us know we must take these moods seriously. All around, wherever I turn, there's the fatal landscape. I won't be able to record this hour, since I'm too poor a painter for that. These fields suck me dry. So my work and I are a singular contradiction.

—Once there was a girl who believed that I had appeared to her in her dream, asking her to go on painting where I had left off. This girl had talent; she wanted to become a painter. Now when I consider that I stopped because there is no going on, then I have to laugh about the girl with that meretricious dream, but on the other hand, I don't know whether I didn't really appear to her in her dream and encourage her to continue. . . . It's possible. Though the likes of us never find successors, the natural creativity of youth sometimes makes us believe in the future, a future that is lost before the night is over. Though I entertain no hope, I believe in the dreaming girl, in her talent, in her reputation, which will ultimately be that of lying in bed with men.

—Those, good sir, are my walks that, should they take place in the city, lead to the neurologist, whom I beg for a strong barbiturate, even though I know he won't prescribe the begged-for poison. So I demand what's outrageous because I'm completely apathetic. The doctor who says no becomes a man whom I trust, one who shies away from me because he's healthy and senses the danger I represent. This danger, which beings like us embody for others, is our great, untimely, burning intensity.

Odd, the Spaniard reflected, that this man whose face reminds me of Vincent, must despair of the power of colors, while what annihilates me is the wall of fog; in both cases a dark death. Thinking about his past, he realized now, if not at some earlier moment, that his stay at the sanatorium had been for nothing. A misstep, but he'd bear it majestically. Marked by a small tree's network of shadows, the beaten man sat there and kept silent or talked, both of which amounted to nothing.

—These endless possibilities for pleasure which increase like the universe itself, from which those who know about them are excluded . . . the Spaniard intoned slowly. But then he suddenly trusted the ruddy man, who for his part seemed to have ended his monologue. Because the landscape all around lay waste, plundered in its fecundity of past harvest autumn, Don Juan began to find words.

—You turn your head and see one of those olive pale faces, like a Spaniard's, like an Italian's, and you go on and don't think, as you once did, that these faces are beautiful. You're standing some place on the corso of the city of Almería quite posssibly, and the intensive bird-song descends on you from the palm trees. You remember the stretch of park in front of the Casino in Monte Carlo where the birds sing even in winter. You think of the oases of Palm Springs, with their yellow and blue hummingbirds. But most of all you think about Monte Carlo, its Casino of bitterness. As you recall, you entered the private gambling room with your beloved escort. She at once became the center of attention, and felt right at home, as she said, while you, who are not at home in gambling halls, who cannot stand coincidences, urged that you leave. Whenever you referred to a light, she, and others, thought they saw darkness; in your life, whenever you mentioned the night, others accused you of denying the light. Through these misunderstandings, you became you.

—You grew old too quickly, and though the world calls you young, young or immortal: it's all the same and cannot delude you as to your real age, even if you are expert in deluding the world, for which you feel no incentive because you're too old.

—You will travel homeward, and once you've reached your six wooden walls, you'll forget the journey more quickly than the journey will forget you. For you must leave tracks behind and you know it, and your enemies will continue to hate you by the traces you leave, as your friends will continue to love you by your traces. You're alone and only your traces find company.

—In Almería, here as everywhere else, you live in an expensive four-star hotel, and from fear of the same sun you used to pursue, you've been sitting for days in the gloomy hotel lobby that's bustling with hollow people. Lost in silence for weeks, you haven't said a word, haven't listened to a word save for the few words with the waiter. In this loud hotel filled with speech, only you are lost in silence. You have the bad habit of muttering to yourself, picked up by degrees, and you're at the mercy of bad habits. Sometimes you address yourself as *thou* and sometimes as *you*: your self-worth varies. You notice how you're slowly going mad, precisely that is what you want to be, even if you deny it in the morning. You live in the expectancy of a modest good fortune: of dwarf-like security in your madness.

—You could step out into the street, onto the broad Corso; you have white shoes and silk suits in your suitcase; you could be the most elegant, the most admired man on the Corso. Like everyone else here, you could take part in the evening stroll: up the Corso on the left, down the Corso on the right, and you could cast lecherous glances like everyone else here. If today, a Tuesday, you went out alone, by tomorrow Wednesday you'd be walking arm in arm with a girl. In love, in heat, like everyone here, you'd be able to forget your past, by repeating it. You could become younger, but you don't want that. You say you'd have to witness all the embraces if you took part. You'd have to see that all over the world men search for women and women for men, for just that one miserable purpose. And you'd have to admit to the lust of children, who become part of our filth here. Watching the young, romantically gilded lovers searching for a bed, you'd have to include their hollow secrets, their banal wonders in your evening stroll. All that would nauseate you today, even though you yourself participated in this charade for eons as one of its most convincing, most famous actors. If you walked the Corso today, you'd have to scale obstacles so high that you would not be walking among people but over rooftops or higher still, namely, in your solitude, which does not pain you, which has become painlessly unbearable. Of all the possibilities, you're off safest in the hotel.

—You're wondering: why? Why did you dine with the world's foremost violinist in San Diego? Why do you listen to La Bohème in English in Glasgow? Why do you love Paris, your oyster of silence? Why do you hire a boy prostitute—Oh how tender he is—in London? Why do you take poison on Capri? And why do you break an engagement in Athens? You settle back in the hotel lobby's easy-chair and don't know the answer. You count your remaining friends and are not amazed. You add up your debts and are not astonished. You order tonic water with ice and lemon from the young waiter, and you can be sure you'll get what you want. Unsure as you are, you have the definite certainty that this waiter will scarcely disappoint you.

—Every night you resolve to return to your room early, to go to bed early. But you never go to bed before two in the morning, and even then you cannot sleep and get up again. You step to the window and see the stars above and the sea below. You see the harbor, the long sea wall with the lighthouse at its farthest end. Beyond that you see the so-called open sea, which remains closed to you however. You would dearly like to go down to the harbor, would like to see the large, rusty ship with the green light on the tip of its mast being pumped dry. Two large pipes suck the oil from the ship's belly into the belly of the harbor wall, into the earth. You would like to stand there and hear the pump pulsing, troubled by no one and heeded by no one, for it is night, for even the sailors are sleeping somewhere now. You want to go down there, but you stay in your room. You're afraid of the vile smells, the harbor's worldly smells, and above all, you're afraid of the many stray dogs here in the south, roving about diseased and ownerless, that die but spread disgust before they die. The sight of mangy dogs, like the sight of begging children, gives you the urge to vomit, because the wretched are repulsive to you, because you feel sorry for the wretched.

—The rooms are air-conditioned; the telephone is beside the bed. Indeed, you never use it, but you feel the security streaming from this telephone into you. You think about the seductive girls who stick like flies to the bar of the Club on the Hotel's ground floor. These girls seduce the men, whereupon the men are called seducers. Unsavory, these people who reduce our world to a bar. But waking or dreaming you see beautiful people, and you think, it would be good to summon them all to my room, but then you think that the beautiful person might be wearing dirty underwear, and already your desire for human contact fades. Your suitcase in your left hand, you walk into an exponentially expanding distance, which becomes too much for you. Interested in your past yet lacking all feeling for it, occasionally puzzled by it, you declare yourself miserably unworthy of your profound puzzlement.

* * *

A unit of disillusionment had been added up here, but how does one measure this unit? In questioning, in silence, in burned-out candles, in drained bottles, in vertiginous escape attempts? How does one measure it? If someone moves his lips only to fall silent again forever, if someone never bothers to say something twice, the listener begins to doubt his listening ears. We doubt whether anything at all was said, or whether in listening we are not being deceived. That is our experience when someone falls silent, be it Jesus or Shakespeare: our ear retains what has been said without knowing what we possess in words. Mankind's greatest sentences crumble in the lightest wind. When great wars and epidemics exterminate whole nations, we count the dead, but don't really believe in their death. It is then that the religion of the fog proclaims its saints, and treacherous is the kiss of faith, the bond to a *thou*.

Naturally, two men like Vincent and Don Juan, had never learned the art of discourse. They were rhetoricians of the soul, dictators in the fields of silence, but their tongues remained awkward and their words were likewise covered in glue. Anyone who bore kinship with these two, who had it in him to have an inkling of understanding of them, should immediately board a train and flee, anywhere. Departure is the only solution, arrival an impossibility.

* * *

Vincent had come from the north, from Amsterdam, where he had visited his museum without being recognized. The pictures he had painted gave him no rest now; rather he was filled with words that he had to express, because all he now was still good for was talking his head off. There's no brush that will fit the hand of a dead man who long ago proclaimed his NO.

—Listen to my words, the ruddy man proposed with evident hesitation, and heed only the words, not their meaning, which becomes blurred even for me. My palette and brush almost understood my glowing colors once, though even then I was painfully aware that so much fire is prohibited. Go to the plains up north that begat me, Don Juan, go there and you'll understand that I'm not risen from the dust but from hell. In the painting with ravens and field there's this dreadful gaping path which no one dares take, since it leads down to the dead.

* * *

—young boys and everything having to do with them: the emptiness, the fullness, the impotence of perfection in the face of the ordinary, the same impotence as ours in the face of the black birds that are careening our way . . . their approach is hell . . .

* * *

—in Amsterdam, I was dismayed by how matter-of-factly people furthest from suicide imputed ordinary or ludicrous motives to the works of a suicide. Olive trees—beautiful faces—painful stars—those are not symptoms of madness, by God, not irresponsible pictures, but natural, ingrown details of my works, not painted, but invisibly ingrown. . .

***

—my wheat fields are riper and richer than anything that can grow on this earth. The harvest, good sir, is automatically denied in these paintings . . .

* * *

—just around the corner, I saw the Château d'Anvers with its blue roof maintain its loyalty to the dream . . . and again wondered how my sowers could expect anything to grow in such earth, beneath such a sun. But it's not a question of growth, neither for the farmer nor for the artist . . .

* * *

—I had to admit defeat. Not even the blossoming trees, these spring pictures that I painted are convincing. Such blossoming in such profusion is painted only by someone who doesn't understand the pain of birth, because he's so obsessed with the pain of dying. . .

* * *

—and then the unavoidable journeys: how many godlike beings wait for the likes of us everywhere, never to be grasped. A life of feverish turning towards people . . . what a task, what a curse. We cannot even manage the first word: we always stammer the last. . .

***

—whatever small comprehension the girls might have, it is covered by lovely loose clothes . . . Pity nonetheless. . . .

* * *

—a former lover's daily letters, understood only so long as you loved . . . since love is understanding . . . and which later went unanswered, un-understood, unread, as love dried up. Death is not a keeping quiet, death is silence. But keeping quiet is hell . . .

* * *

—I visited friends: the painters and singers and humanists near my museum, had tea with them and thought: yes. Yes. . . yes to Charlotte who was murdered by the Nazis . . . And yes even to life. But painting: what for? . . .

* * *

—nevertheless became absorbed the same day in my snowy landscape of Saint Rémy, in this emerald cold. As I saw young men in short-sleeved shirts standing in front of the work, I knew they didn't understand my painting: they weren't freezing. Whoever conveyed such cold could give joy to the viewer. Warmth—for joy is warmth—through cold. . .

* * *

—went weeping to Kalverstraat. When people take their leave, take the first few steps—how heart-rendingly quick they are. They take the first steps and are already so far away from us that if they turned around, they could never reach us again. That's how far you are after only a few steps. Reasons for suicide, good sir. . . .

* * *

—why suicide? A childish question. Dying, wherever you look death is waving to you. Lovers walk arm in arm: it's shocking and, for the saint, lovely to see that they have all found one another and that there's no place left for the seeker to arrive at. . . .

* * *

—the pilgrimage into my dark life. At first, people will have to resign themselves to the fact that I was a human being, an ugly fellow, someone who sat in pubs at tables without table-cloth. People have to remember my corporeality; they should be prepared to run into me at any moment. Only then can they be absorbed in my art without doing me an injustice. But I'm used to injustice. I used to paint with the same lassitude and breathlessness with which all of us go under. The first impression depends on quantity, then perhaps on the shabby rest, on quality, that's how the world draws its balance sheet. . .

* * *

—the question is raised during the dastardly day whether the vast blue of my skies is a matter of warmth or of cold. . .

* * *

—and slowly I realize that my eyes could not lie, that my eyes were extremely sad. . . .

* * *

—in Amsterdam, I was a visitor of that museum just like the others. But toward evening, when the sun broke through the glass panes of this modern building, it was clear to me that there's no one left alive who could still record this singular sun's everyday uniqueness . . . and I found brown leaves everywhere. They fall and lie in the path. You walk across them thoughtlessly, but some of us will be buried beneath those leaves . . .

* * *

—death's memorable distinctions. . .

* * *

—time and again I rushed to my chair with candle and book. All my life I said yes to grief, but how insignificant this grief becomes when I stare at my canvases for any length of time . . . American girls stand beside me, studying the picture. They're young and momentarily their soft hair gives the lie to my artistry. But when this moment has passed, the girls have become old and stringy; they no longer give me the lie. . .

* * *

—I am the only one who has heard the canvas of these paintings crumble in rhythm with our death. No difference and no victory in that, and no improvement. . .

* * *

—I am disgusted by those who marvel at my room in Arles and utter the lie: how simple, how beautiful! Not one of these hypocrites would want to call my room's simplicity his own. . .

* * *

—often, especially among the violet trees, I feel like a stage prop: that is when I am at my most honest. In some paintings I become the priest that I never became. . .

* * *

—don't want to bore you further, Don Juan. It's a consolation that I was allowed to experience the light and the summer before the brightness overwhelmed and annihilated me. Before long, let me tell you, the radiance of my paintings will melt the frames and turn the paints into a foul-smelling sauce. Brightness is not intensified light but visible darkness. Light would be mild . . . more than that I shouldn't say . . .

* * *

—we both know it's easier to receive a kiss than an understanding word. These were the impressions, Don Juan, that I took away with me from Amsterdam and, intimidated by my life and driven into flight, not accepted hospitably by my death, I reached this path and you, caballero. I thoroughly doubt whether the two of us can help each other. If you'll permit, we'll rise and go our way. We've given each other what every encounter must eventually become: a refuse dump. Like me, you're in lighter spirits now, and the evening is drawing near. If we go at once, you this way and I that, we'll be able to cover a good stretch before dark. And since the world keeps getting larger, there's hardly any danger that we'll see each other again. This near-certainty strikes me as decisive, for if we met again, we'd both have to blush for shame; we'd be terribly embarrassed. Two tragedies have destined us for solitude: that the encounter strips us completely, and that we're ashamed once we are naked.

CHAPTER IV

At moments when he felt ill and tried aspirin to stifle an oncoming cold he became aware that physical is decidedly worse than mental pain, which we usually only imagine. Sweat on his brow, his mouth dry, he lay fully clothed on his bed, looking out the window. I hope I won't get ill, he almost prayed to himself; an illness now of all times would ruin everything.

He attached sufficient worth to every second of his increasingly empty life to consider it indispensable. The wind, which engaged the trees in front of the house in dancing motions during these hours, struck him as that very monster solely responsible for time and death; and he nourished an increasingly distinct feeling that he had to to be like the wind to extend his past for as long as was humanly possible. To acquire the necessary permanence of his existence, which consisted of moods notions, and pains, Don Juan hit upon literature.

Yet he had never become a literary person. His efforts had invariably remained fragmentary, but since he had abandoned the seduction of bodies and set out on an exploratory journey into his longing, his strength now hardly sufficed for the strain of writing fragments. Of course, it was not merely his aging and the related ebbing of strength that were to blame; it was rather that things resist being recorded, that only the especially strong and ruthless man can manage the occasional page, which instantly and haplessly entangles you in guilt. Nonetheless, it seemed to him that the gates to the world of the spirit lay open only to sensuality, pure literature belonged to the sullied author. When a life becomes sterile, art too, becomes sterile.

It was not Don Juan's style to be going around telling stories. He despised those who invented their books. To be sure, there are no rules or conditions for a story's truth, and the story that occurs only in the mind is just as true as another that takes place in the street. He knew that as well as anyone. But the "only in your head story" hardly satisfies, because we are born with senses and because we demand something to lay our hands on, demand bodies in space, demand breathing bodies, demand human beings that breathe. It had taken Don Juan much time to accept the body as the seat of the soul, and this insight wore on him. He observed coolly how others found their way, blindly or knowingly, around in this world of bodies, without being able to develop any genuine understanding for that dimension of breathing. Blind or knowing: Don Juan restrained his laughter.

For Don Juan, blindness meant the bridge between grace and curse—humanity in its most natural form—whereas sight was the sloth's alternative, the non-path as such. It had taken Don Juan centuries to grasp that the world did not revolve around the sun, but around man and woman who sleep with each other. It had taken the great seducer centuries to find out with his head what we normally do at eighteen. The secret of his life was the twofold unity of his inhibitions, which held him back from any close contact; secondly, his reputation as the widely feared and envied seducer, the downfall of men and women, boys and girls, dangerous in his mystical twainness of innocence and sin—even as God in His Trinity is dangerous for man.

Christ or Don Juan, Francis of Assisi or Gilles de Rais: such are the earth's agonizing titles of nobility, terrestrial and yet not formed of dust, godlike as the bodies of men who abandon themselves to everything, whose faith is their lack of loyalty. Being human means being what we are, and above that stands the consolation of lust and the consolation of death. By the time Don Juan had acquired this insight, time had sufficiently jaded him to let him pass over this piece of wisdom with a shrug of his shoulders. He had reached the age when you participate in everything, when our heads become Janus-faced, adjustable without movement.

There flared up again his childhood habit of closing his eyes and pressing the lids tight for as long as he could manage. Yet in this newly attained darkness he saw no internal images, but only a black, velvety cloth whose purpose was easily guessed. At one time Don Juan had written poetry under various names, but his incredible sensitivity had eventually turned him against lyricism. Once he used to read at three in the morning, dine, satisfy a woman; now he was dead-tired by midnight. His fatigue grew to the extent that his compassion for human beings grew.

Yes, compassion and fatigue, and a measure of nausea increasingly moved him to rash and mean actions which discouraged him. Thus he threw a valuable coin at a beggar woman who had tried out a faded melody on her mouth-organ but he had looked the other way as he did so. Not until he went on did he realize how worthless this valuable gift had been, since his refusal to look had insulted the woman in the beggar. In this world it was decidedly easier to find a bedmate than an understanding look. Vincent had been quite right . . .

But most of the time Don Juan avoided thoughts of that kind—cogitating was just too tiresome for him. A certain senility had seized on him, which related nicely to the many centuries he had lived, but it startled him nonetheless. Thus Don Juan dragged himself through time and literature, even through this book, without finding a starting point for action. He couldn't teach himself the act of surrender, he wasn't writing his autobiography; he was stumbling across the threshold to himself, and he denied himself—a saint even in that—a *thou* or a *we*. Only the *I* existed for Don Juan, a twisted, lost *I*.

On one of the coldest winter days, filled with the yearning to be like a crystal, he stammered the prayer of atonement, a prayer that only he knew, which welled syllable by syllable from his blue discolored lips.

perhaps
a furtive grasp
for evening-
the fear
of icy stars
has come of age

the "thou" leads
to no light
that might yet bend
a stiff neck

but it sings
of the distinct green
of never dared attempts.

And already Don Juan was nearer to the growth of trees. Already he was gathering documents for *his* Death in Venice.

It mattered to keep his composure now, and not to be amazed—amazement ruins so much. For it can happen that you feel absolutely like nothing for weeks, months on end, that you are nothing: incapable of thought, unworthy of a single written line, so that you walk alongside your life into a darkness that can neither be lightened by love nor by the tenderness of Athens's evening sky. Not every one in that state is saved by an encounter; for loyalty is one thing, but to be too tired, too timid for new love is a bad sign . . . And though I am supposed to drink that dark pomegranate juice—which is just *Bitter San Pellegrino*—to drink it slow, drink it to satisfy death's slowness—if it is late, long after midnight, the glass should still be full—I slurp the stuff down; forced in this as in every instance to race, to this frenzied impatience that might lead death to suppose that I fear him. For I tremble, outwardly, in the face of death and his precision.

* * *

It can happen that a man must keep silent who usually says only important things, that he betrays his gift of speech and wastes his customary precision, and then sets out shamelessly on the ways of mediocrity. There—hot in his appetite for young bodies—he feels he is on the way back: the return to his actual task. Tree, palm or just a bush, but—in any case—something with roots, a return to the anchor that was cast into the calm harbor. Where Someone said "rise, and go forth!" someone else might say "be yourself again." If you are saved in that fashion, how should you respond? Should you kneel down on the sidewalk beside the shop's ugly wares, in the salty stench of the pedestrians, who keep their distance now: unwanted, recognizable again in their nullity, only now truly shockingly naked . . . or should you continue on in this hour of reawaking, walk on to the silent terrace where you feel the magnificent coolness which you want to live . . . No question marks.

* * *

The freshness of a terrace which does not betray its former guests in any way, whose discretion a suicide and a lover can trust. Distantly I recall myself as the dandy who seduced the boy on the terrace—the thought elicits no strong feeling, only thirst. And for the umpteenth time I order the dark Pomegranate juice, or is it *Bitter San Pellegrino*, whose freshness makes me become present to myself.

Those shrilly lighted days come back to me when I was looking in this hotel for the object of my lust on the lido which, finding it, I did not find. For eight hundred years I tore the clothes off the backs of young bodies, I sought sin but found purity, found the shy nakedness of the pale and the suntanned. I make believe that I enjoyed the centuries while I created the drama of filth. I, the director of fading childhood, of the seemingly dying youth, I, Don Juan, remained long enough in Venice to learn the pleasure you can take in water, water and watery corpses, in inescapable loneliness during the search for my first love.

* * *

Disgusted by poverty and nauseated by wealth, blind to moderation, allergic to extremes, bored by bodies and scarcely all there in the spirit, I no longer understand that premature decision, that immature YES which I kept shouting to others. I no longer understand my commitments, berate myself eternally stupidly so. Each and every word during my terrible eight hundred years was an ALWAYS. This word was the evil temptation and deadly poison of my language until necessity shut it up. Don Juan was a fool for EVER AND ALWAYS, someone who had to keep abandoning himself, someone who—contrary to public opinion—

also accepted into his bargain the fairness of wages of pain, bore them, collected them . . . swilled the collection around in his mouth till he needed a shot of madness to cleanse his throat, to open it for the seed of the youngsters whom I met.

* * *

Tiberius' "little fishes," details of Gothic cathedrals, sunbeams on the disrobed bodies, details: the way crabs crawl backwards at the beach, suicide plans, and always something literary alongside the main vantage line, the windless, waveless line that guided me into Vincent's burning fields so as to break off there: palpitations, a quick decline.

CHAPTER V

—You have all the sensual complications, but you are not adept in spiritual matters.

The sentence comes at me from a letter; the sentence comes from him. In reply, I write these pages, these thousand stories which are missing the one important story. I'll assume that we exist. I'll surmise that what we experienced is true, and I'll chain my doubts.

Only a few days ago we ate dinner in the open, under the arcades on the Place des Vosges. It took time for us to make the delicate choice of our meal, and by the time we decided, the sun had set. We called the waiter and changed our order; because of the twilight we asked for bright dishes and a sunny wine. If it isn't one thing, it must be the consolation of the other. The waiter passed our capricious order on to the kitchen, which complied. In the clear evening we sat on the Place des Vosges and spoke German. It was our last conversation.

Before then we'd often met, had traveled from afar to this Place des Vosges, with its wicker chairs, its crooked tables, to be together and ill at ease for an evening. We usually came in May or June when the days are generous. Though each time we imagined that we had changed, at our first words we realized how unchanged we were.

Then a year had passed, and our meeting went as it had gone the last time. As we ate, we mutely tested each other, but by the time we got to the Camembert, we knew the score. We didn't hold the stand-off against each other. We weren't your average patient, each wanting to be more ill than the other, each of course wanting to survive. We'd already survived; we had already survived and survived the others according to schedule. We possessed a gracious form of immortality, it was ours like an inherited jewel. After the annual meal we would part and spend one more night in Paris—at most; and in the morning we would board the first train to make our way home, to escape; on separate tracks. He, who lives in Germany, who was first to write after each meeting (who cast the first stone), passed up the lastingness that might have been, whereas I, who received these letters, who lived anywhere but in Germany, got burnt in my search for the lasting.

—What bothers me in Paris, he often said, is the time you spend just on living here.

In the early morning, he'd board the train which swarmed with slovenly travelers and Germans. Who after all leaves from the Gare du Nord? The good trains, which arrive mornings amid flowers, leave the Gare de Lyon, the Gare d'Austerlitz, in the evening. These are the stations of the chosen few, even if homesick beggars do sleep in their halls. What bothered him in Paris, was the time it took to live. So for some, time is too valuable for life, whereas for our kind, life is too precious for time. But the guests around us at the Place des

Vosges knew nothing about that. If you go among the people only in the summer, you're forgotten, of course. We were served with the same chill reserve that we showed each other. Only rarely did we shake hands.

For all that, lust had once streaked meteorically between the boy and myself. It was a nebulous eroticism—it was acknowledged but not indulged. Once we headed the car for the vacant forest clearing, but the autumn air of Salzkammergut was much too chaste; and one time we slept in the same bed, because a second one was not to be found in all of Paris. We never touched. This unintentional but still powerful and agonizing abstinence aged both of us. One Monday we awoke from our ephebic dream, saw the hair on our legs, and retreated into the shell that each had held ready all along. This twinlike development came to pass on its own, of course, within Germany and outside, and if we did dine once a year, we did not discuss it. What hurt me was his growing up. Thus everything that's in the singular here could be in the plural. It would be as child's play to place a mirror on the opposite side and thus to repeat these phrases in the reverse order of their meaning.

If, at the Place des Vosges, we noticed and diagnosed our stand-off without amazement, we yet silently knew about the long after-dinner walk we owed each other. We looked forward to it like children. Now I don't walk through our Paris any more. No longer do I walk through Paris, since the evenings have become night rags wound about my blindness. After settling the bill at the restaurant, we got on our way. Every step and every stop were appointed by our fore-pleasure. We couldn't say whether we were anticipating future or repeating earlier walks. But one thing had changed: our once easy pace, the initial headlong rushing had become a leaden, laborious drag. I found myself invariably lagging several steps behind him. Thusly we made our way into the ways of the night, like worms we burrowed forward, singly and together. The world was rich with obstacles. We kept walking until we reached the ingrown alleys of the Marais, finally down the Rue Vieille du Temple, walked past the door of number 47 which stuck out its tongue at us, past what was slowly dying, and then made our tortuous way over to Ile Saint-Louis. We sent glances up along softly lit façades where—wherever you looked—there gaped those large uncurtained windows with books and pictures behind them. As if only good people who used their minds lived on this island, friends whom we simply just never ran into . . . certainly only the summer gave rise to such thoughts. In the frost and rain these windows would scorn whoever stared up at them.

Then we reached Notre Dame, which was his passion, not mine. He always lingered there, annually discovered new stone dragons, sandstone snakes never seen before, gargoyles again and again. Always a few steps ahead of me, he would celebrate his chaste, Gothic orgies in the empty night streets, as I stood by, polite and impatient.

We all wear the magic coat, only it doesn't transform everyone in the same way. Owning it doesn't mean you can fly; some of us only get heavier in it. Then the German was in his Germany again, he, the feverishly cold man, writing letters . . . He had a slightly better idea of ghosts, he, who lived in the land of ghosts, and I was on the Champs Elysées, reading his letters. Each probably smiled about the other, he about me and I about him. German letters, chameleon letters: the ink changes color and turns to blood.

But on our nightly excursions we both avoided the Champs Elysées: this street is simply too narrow for two—it opens up solely for the solitary walker. There the stars that hardly anyone sees go pale; there the tight midnight clothes in which no dead man would allow himself to be resurrected gesture at you. The solitary walker who walks beneath those trees will be in a strange mood. He reads these letters and feels tempted to say, *Unter den Linden*, because to his mind this name is no less bright than Champs Elysées, and because, here as there, you encounter the same grotesques,the same impossibility of living.

So I walked, ambled, saw skin-tight clothes, saw the childlike lust that makes us hot, but that in a wink changes its objects into mannequins: two dead cylinders for thighs, arched nothing for hips, blue glass for eyes, pink plastic for skin. Then I ran from the taped voices, ran ran until I was alone: I could take renewed pride in not having needed anyone. I was in Paris and had lost all desire.

Traveling on separate tracks, we became used to a life of innocence. In our stand-off, we had relinquished all movement; even the warmth of spring burnt us. But the guests in the restaurant did not see through us, the Place des Vosges did not even take notice of us. On the basis of this universal indifference we established our annual meal, our love, the stand-off, the final break.

Back into the first person singular—to save space, for the world as we know is too small. Whoever discovers himself as he reads along: go take the mirror, go decipher the world of reversed pages. As for me, I write, note down the plan, stake out the field, am at work, am not with you. It's late, almost too late to begin. I'm beginning too late in the year and too late in the years. If on a summer's day we manage it through to evening without a thunderstorm, and change our clothes before going down to dinner—then this has the taste of a victory. Our last supper in the Place des Vosges, where we sought to efface our past and our origins mouthful by mouthful, drink by drink.

The summer day had reached its apogee. The colors were vibrant, yet silence, mercifully, lay over everything. I sat there, the letter in my hands, waiting. I began to understand: I was waiting for a sigh, so was the broad tree, everything was waiting. But a sound presupposes emptiness. It can resound where there are no people. The shadow kept describing its arc. Should I go back to the house? I saw how nothing had changed, saw how nothing would change. The conviction about the impossibility of any and all goals struck me as the engine for action.

Consider how quickly the fires are extinguished, how rashly we act. There was a time when we let no day go by without visiting the graves. Not so long ago we kneeled in the filthy snow and kissed the patches of bare earth. This childish obstinacy not to accept the death of those who are dead, not to believe in their death, and thereby to wrong the dead, since they have earned our trust by not having lied to us when they were alive . . . Now we spend weeks in our city, totter along the thousand alleys, glance, however seldom, toward the cemetery but can't even find the entrance. Even if the faces change, if they follow another like the links of a chain, we should nonetheless divide love into its rooms, the night of love with the dead ought not to be an orgy. Our bodies, our souls, which we comb through anew each day, and which nevertheless seem unfamiliar to us, that we forget much too quickly. . . .

We were well served by the girl's dying, not impoverished. Only when she lay dead on the street did the streets come alive, sucking blood into asphalt pores, blossoming, propelling wheels, stirring up the pedestrians' wild longing for new bereavements. A fair trade: a person had lived and has bled to death but her blood breathes life into that paltry future which is our present now.

Don Juan ought to know where youth hides out. Youth does not have many hiding places, there are cemeteries and there is life, two narrow fenced in cheap arenas where no one escapes the other.

* * *

Although the dead girl's mother, whom loss

and suffering kept rejuvenating, this woman, who still carried the body of a girl from whom so much life and already so much death had issued, although this mother possessed sufficient warmth to provide some consolation, it was the three boys, the dead girl's brothers, the dead girl's gift to me, this threefold single perfection, that—in its trinity—proved death's impotence to me. Each of the three was equally worthy of love, and their plusses and minuses were rendered meaningless by the fact that they were three. Although love as a subtle form of possessiveness was inconceivable in this ghostly family, everyone's affection was devoted to the littlest, who returned this warmth manifold. For us it was an incomprehensible blessing that, while we ourselves grew older, slipping and dying away, this boy remained the same for a long, if limited, period of time; cuddly, filled with sadness and joy, with an inner light, a kind companion to us who were growing darker. At the same time Thomas, the most beautiful of the boys, grew taller and more tender as he grew, and as we dined, as I spoke, or worse, dictatorially did all the talking, Thomas fixed his gaze on me. With his large eyes he looked at me until I blushed with embarrassment. Thomas who smiled as he blushed in turn, seemed as if he wanted to say: "Yes, you may well talk, since you're unsure of yourself, but there's actually no reason to even speak." And George, the eldest (whom every movement in the world made paler and more distinguished) was with us too. Only later, when he suddenly turned gray, unable to conceal his weakness any longer, did this family's precious and fragile unity become completely apparent to me. That is what Europe was like, as difficult, beautiful, and consecrated for death. Then we paid quickly and left the restaurant to take the eldest and exhausted son back home. This almost uncanny turn took place with the calm and dignity of every tragedy that befell this family, and with the devotion of those who stand at a distance from illness. Then there were my shy embraces, my kisses wrested from my sense of my incompetence, and much hope for blessings, lacking conviction: bless them all; don't *You* see who must be safe-guarded here?

Then I drove to another country and, as always after such encounters, felt unsure of my painstakingly achieved position, cast out from calm into new unrest, a new desire, a new tempest. I almost forgot that there was nothing to be lamented here, that there was only occasion for joy. To love the other side and to maintain your own side, that's what mattered, and to see the growth of the younger ones with all the good suspense that our relinquishment has been ordained to weave into this world. There followed nights of deep sleep, and today those days strike me like an answered prayer . . .

Since then I've come to realize that love deserves to be protected, that it should be fostered and—according to our distorted dimensions—immortalized, which is possible only in calmness. All memory should be topographically arranged, and the future . . . there is no future.

For how else could our human bonds have been able to withstand so much ugliness, vile eruptions from the harmonious frame, and have reached equilibrium again, and how could these bonds have been preserved, how could we have survived, if some indestructable plan did not inhere in life. For life not so much acquires meaning with growing awareness as nobility. A young person had to die for us to find each other, but this encounter already negated the leave-taking. We know that no one is dead, and we live with a painfully fatiguing intensity which is only granted to those who stand close to the abyss. Something dreadful is crawling toward us; we don't know what, but surmise sleepily that this evil, however it may appear, will fit in and be part of our speechless life.

CHAPTER VI

The Slow Transition to Mourning

In the evening, as we drove past the rusty signpost, I found myself seized by that trembling that proved to me again how unreal my painstakingly achieved maturity was. The certainty with which I traversed my space whose boundaries were far more tightly drawn than I care to admit was only a seeming certainty. The cosmopolite lived on feet of clay, did not live in accordance with his rank, but in the oppressive valley of his human origin. Were not beginning and end of all sensation to be found in this saint—*San Floriano*—who protected this village, and whose name, though richly laden, had not always been sacred for me: despite its weight it belonged to the best, the most valuable that my life had to show?

Perhaps I reduced my car's speed for the fragment of a minute, but beyond that I didn't let my consternation show, which came easy to me, since I'm a master of concealment. The woman with me had certainly overlooked the signpost: *San Floriano.* She hadn't read the name or, if she had, there was no way she would be sufficiently familiar with it to sit up and take notice. But struck by the syllables, I suddenly asked myself why this young woman, whom I pretended to love, whom I had persuaded myself I loved, was sitting beside me. Why we were driving to Siena together was no longer so obvious, and that we shared a bed at night suddenly struck me as a wicked betrayal; though who was betraying whom in this hollow union I would have been unable to say. Nor did I believe that I owed anyone anything. But even if my betrayal had been only of my commitment to solitude, it would also have been an inexcusable offense against the rusty name. I even went so far as to question this woman's right to drive past the *San Floriano* signpost with me. My companion had no business in this landscape: Umbria was a land of victorious mourning, not made for a creature which laughed about the sense of dying, who fell asleep in the car, who doesn't read rusty signposts. If only a few minutes before I would have resisted such exaggerated accusations, dismissing them as arbitrary because I found them unjust, now they seemed justified, and my mind was brimming with them. The more we love women the more they despise us. I had to berate myself for having wasted an ocean of time with this blind person, although since the rusty name neither time nor togetherness were permitted anymore.

Our journey was madness, vertiginous madness. We raced from city to city, from loathing to loathing; I wanted to stay, she wanted to go on. While I was obsessed with my fatigue, she was obsessed with her hunger, which had nothing to do with youth and restlessness, but with hatred for warmth and hatred of light. ln her eyes I was the brilliant one, she did not want to see the sun but wanted shadowy people. But I had followed her; her flight became our life together, became hell, completely made up, with arrivals at quiet hotels, with silent dinners with scented candles. So far I hadn't let her go—her: that contradiction in the white dress—because I wanted her body to help me forget the rusty name, and this despite the fact that *San Floriano* was nothing, not a way out and no obligation any longer, not a hope and, for a long time, not even a dream. It was a rusty signpost raised in front of a row of dilapidated houses where it is not recommended you stop. The great majority of human settlements allows the likes of us nothing but to drive through at excessive speed. Even racing through them like this stirs the urge to vomit, whereas stopping in these villages would mean death. But now I felt occasion to apply the brakes and tell my companion: Get out: you're free. But she would not have been free, would have stood alone on the street, waiting for a new attachment. When normal people encounter a mind, they retain a talent for stepping down, a knack for bankruptcy when the irridescent affair is over.

As I remember, all she wanted to do was dance; she'd always loved dancing, yet when she fell in with me, she had to realize that dancing with me was out of the question. Always I remained a mountain for her, immovable, however moved internally, and what was worse for her: I was a magnetic mountain. Only once did I give in to her and agree to go dancing. We went to a discotheque but then sat quietly at a table, ordered drinks and did not dance, while the others stalwartly danced. It was quite dark in the hall; the light was just enough to see the bodies, these whirling obstacles as you danced, barely enough to avoid collisions, though everyone in the hall was bent on collision and fusion. But no desire for dancing was left in her, who had for years begged me for a night of dancing. Come, let's dance, I said, come on, but she refused. I became louder, more insistent, angry; became an object of her dislike, I, the non-dancer, the centuries old man, I, who never danced . . . You probably want to dance with others . . . with younger men, with better dancers with better skin . . . but she burst into tears. So we drove back to the hotel where she disappeared tearfully into the bathroom. If I recall correctly, that was the night we stopped kissing good-night forever, to this day.

Since she knows me, dancing has meant nothing but sadness for her. I'm accused of having destroyed her naiveté, her talent in joy; of being a murderer. How ridiculously weak the murdered are.

We reached Lake Trasimeno. It was winter and the sun was just setting. The water lay like magic before us. It was not the great dare of depth that spoke from the rippling lake, but the lake's totality that revealed itself, a summa that had been kept intact over the summer. I slowed down and looked. The lake, this evening, this land were rich and enriching, let the *San Floriano* signpost go and rust; the name was written in the air; everywhere I found the soft name. In my thoughts I drove through its syllables into this lake, not a single woman's body refreshed like it.

She, my companion, was sleeping now, and she was not missed. Her head had settled onto her right shoulder and looked much too young. Her youth incensed me; this was not permissible. One glance into this evening, a single glance makes you old. But she slept, overslept, missed out, remained young.

The evening glow trusted the sleeping woman's closed eye lids with southern light-headedness. Without asking for dignity and readiness, it poured the velvet that I love so anxiously over the girl's eyes—I was already feeling sorry for her. I needed her again, if not for herself, then much rather as part of the cypress-overgrown shores to which she too belonged. Encouraged by the day's last glimmers, I put my free hand lightly on the sleeper's brow: "wake up, look how beautiful!"

She was to have her share of the light going to sleep. But she grumbled: leave me be, can't you see I'm tired, I don't want to see anything . . . and she fell asleep again. In what direction, I asked mutely, do people sleep? Only hatred bears sleep's mask for no one should confuse sleep with peace. Sleep is absence.

The stars appeared and left the lake to itself. The great reed surrounded body knew what transpired in the dark, knew it better than I, Don Juan, the driver who had to hold the wheel for the gruesomely sleeping woman, even at night. I sped further west toward the slopes of Siena.

Once arrived in this non-city, which bears the name of the most colorful death, I granted my companion's wish for separate rooms for the first time. Even if I hoped, initially, that this arrangement would last no longer than a single night, I knew I could not allow the separation to cause me any pain in the event that it was for good. My body didn't need her's any longer, and I was too old for pride in love. I would sleep alone again, as I had as a child, and my solitary, wintry freezing would be the echo of the bells.

Each of us dragged his weary body into its respective solid four walls to fall asleep without lust or to lie awake without desire. We wanted to be able to look into each other's eyes the following morning without being bewildered by a night full of lust without tenderness. Too much between us had become ordinary: We desperately needed separate rooms to create the physical distance that, unfortunately, we couldn't achieve within ourselves. My companion had made a clever request: for that remoteness which promises the cold.

Finally alone in my room, I greeted my Siena again, which had changed little since the great drama of death had played there in the times of the plague: through the open window I saw the red roofs, I was freezing and still saw the rusty signpost before my eyes, read and reread and practiced saying the name *San Floriano*, whom I suddenly needed anew. But then I closed the window and adjusted myself to having finally attained self-sufficiency. Siena was well suited for thinking, suited for insomnia, for hand-carried diseases, to taking delight in bleeding losses.

But my companion of course misused the city. She was wide awake, didn't stay in her room, merely changed clothes, freshened up, made herself magical, and—I heard the door creaking—left the hotel by herself. She was right to go out, to go where there were people, to let herself be taken, for she needed glamour and abduction. My companion was attached to colors without being able to paint and she adhered helplessly to beauty, without being beautiful.

I turned towards the wall, and surrendered passionately to my love of being alone.

Of the weight
of a newly cast
No

Foams up
your loneliness
that peaceful glider

Later
when everyone
loses his speech
thirstily staring
into some face.

CHAPTER VII

Dreamed Morning and Remembrance

Because that yearning that we cannot follow can become all too real for us, Don Juan awoke at the first light of this January day and was seized by desire for the sun. Still too caught up in the night to be able to just shake off his fatigue with ease, unsure of the new day's successful outcome, Don Juan left his wide bed and began a summer's day. Perhaps it was foolish to give up the heat of the woman still sleeping at his side and to step out of the protective covers into the room's cold. He had luxuriated in the woman's warmth all night, and at certain moments—they slept in the nude—he had been unable to suppress a slight excitement, but he had left the young mother's sleep undisturbed. During the initial phase of their union they had "tamed" each other nearly without let-up; but that "taming," as they smilingly called their "sleeping together," was now over. Besides, the sleeping woman needed her rest since she had become a mother and her back ached far too often and her circulation was erratic. This poor Ophelia required a lot of care, and he granted her her rest.

He limited the "taming" to those occasions when she herself asked for it, and he also helped the mother with her responsibilities for the child.

Yet he was startled by the perfection of the small creature, which was already eleven months old, and whose growing fingernails and comprehending eyes stood in such stark contrast to its muteness. Though natural for its age, the infant's lack of words pained him. Supplied with the books and latest findings about child care, the "parents" knew perfectly well what to do, if only imperfectly so. They watched, as their care bore fruit, how the child had allegedly developed more quickly than other infants its age, but these little triumphs, though they fed the mother's pride, left Don Juan feeling indifferent. He couldn't really grasp his being a father, felt that he was only playing the role of father, but for the time being he was playing his role well.

He would have preferred the child not to begin screaming so early each day, screaming for milk; even before seven o'clock Don Juan rushed into the kitchen to fill the plastic bottle with milk. And there he saw the dirty dishes from the previous day and wondered whether he should wash them; it would have been a pretty gesture on his part, but he decided against it. For that was not why he had risen, he who, if it came to that, would still be asleep at noon. To be washing dishes at seven in the morning is blasphemy, and that was one sin he did not want to commit, and so he went into the nursery and stuffed the bottle into the screaming child's mouth.

Don Juan completed his morning toilet more quickly than usual, in less than three minutes, as if he were a boy washing himself. Yet Don Juan should have washed off a good many things; his washing was not child's play, was perhaps hardly feasible anymore. Even this marriage game he was engaged in: like always, he was searching for but not finding—now in this union—himself. What a presumption: Don Juan as another's partner! Then the purpose of his ablution was again the rusty name, which at times suggested piano études and incense, the love of marzipan acolytes and a sugary voluptuousness that illsuit a husband. Nothing suited Don Juan, the seeker; even his search hardly suited him.

Dressed now, Don Juan re-entered the bedroom to admire the perfection of his sleeping wife's skin. The blanket had slipped from her and to the floor. Don Juan placed the blanket and spread his yearning for summer gently over the resting woman. On this unusual yet ordinary morning, he had lapsed into a literary mood, and with paper and pencil he went out to the balcony.

Leading a literary life does not mean writing, but release from the overwhelming warmth of bodies and from the frosty January air. Being everywhere and nowhere, disdaining and admiring yourself, being a god with complexes, that is what it means to live the literary life, a literary mood. And as in music, this "mood" has nothing to do with being moody, but with the foundation of a possible world.

Don Juan's disdain for the people he saw rushing to work from his balcony did not detract from his admiration for pretty hair and exciting legs. More lust resides in disdain than in dignity. Don

Juan, who loved to stroke his chin, suddenly discovered two hairs left over after shaving. To remove them at once struck him as the most important thing in the world now, more important than that literary mood in which, as he would never forget, all other moods lie embedded. Don Juan went into the bathroom and reflected on his age. It was late, unspeakably late. He would write but his first line was not set until he had completed his second shave.

* * *

When I am sitting alone by the beach and reach out for the reachable but it remains unreachable, then the noiseless sleepers play ball behind me. Sometimes a cry cuts through the air, not from vultures at my back but from ugly children whom the sun has done no favors except for dark hair, dark eyes. I stretch out my hands again for the soul's gentle faces. The beauty of people—it forges through our lives: a beam that lays our illnesses bare. Now we're aware of our sorrows; we bury the fickle story. There's an ocean in front of the house. The fishermen with their woolen caps are looking for a quick catch; for a long time now, they haven't carried off a siren, a mermaid, but they have wives at home who cook and wait and lie down at night. Sailors measure the sea in pesos, in drachmas, in pounds. Yet the seas also carry messages in a bottle, though rarely are they like gentle faces: letters that don't complain of distress at sea or on islands, lines not sent by Robinson, but for the likes of us who return home to find nothing but a white-washed room that will have to do until morning.

When I'm with people I forget the many dead faces. Although the shrill voices outshrill each other, I slow down the course of history with excuses about godly lust, about sensual obsession with truth, about the wisdom of excess. So the pigs are served well by having studied: they illuminate the night with what they've learned; they reduce the light to a common nauseous denominator.

Waiting periods in concert halls, the indifferent church naves of forests, a thousand pictures in galleries. If some good-for-nothing came along now and affixed old German or new American names or, dictionary-like, provides the cheapest names, then all we'd need would be a dusty carnival cart, and basta! we'd have our *commedia dell'arte.* Four wheels on the cart and a hole pierced into the curtain to see whether everyone's there . . . But what does it matter; we're living today and we sometimes play to an empty house . . . So let's risk a glance through the curtain, take three deep breaths, but be careful: don't take your first entrance from the left; that would spell disaster, and someone must be responsible, for example the poet himself, if no one else, and the play can begin, with uncertainty, for no one really knows who's playing good and who evil . . .

Then sudden hiccups, that sounds so cute, the dreadful event that ruins every actor's appearance. Indisposed, I'm lying in bed; I hardly dare eat. I never open the window, for fear of the ugly flies. I lie naked on the bed, the covers drawn back, and I keep my eyes closed, disgusted by my own body. On my way, during my trip to the bathroom, I have to pass the large mirror in which I see my body and I say: so that's I, and immediately afterwards: no, that's not me. All narcissism has been sloughed off; what remains is someone who could say a thing or two, but who remains silent. It's my own fault that I'm so alone, but what is guilt in the face of endless solitude?

I step back into the room and see the still sleeping woman. On our way we must have strayed into an unfamiliar galaxy, which means that an endless amount of time has passed. After these nights together, when we turn to each other and turn away again, trying to sleep face to face or back to back, startled by the touch of a hot or cold arm around our hips, fleetingly think about squids, then drift off into thoughts about the lukewarm, half-hearted certainty of our marriage, our connectedness, we fall asleep again while the child is in the other room: pretends to lie in the other room, because, actually, the child is draped as a dark canopy across our bed. The child is audibly sucking its bottle which is filled with our blood. I feel dead in the morning, and my wife, no, this girl runs from the room and fetches the child. Then she speaks to the vigorous creature while I am lying half-asleep, and I hear nothing, barely make out the smacking of lips, sad church bells from outside which tell me that our cycle is completed, that the stars are in the rear. Then the mother chases me out of bed for the child to play in.

I want to return to my past. Nothing worth remembering happened there. Nothing could have happened: time was against us. The encounter with my shell, with Don Juan was invariably short-lived, without the weightiness of a fateful outward occurrence. Life exhausted itself in moronic presence; experiences drowned in it.

Our bounds were strictly set. They incise the growth of this friendship with Janus-faced silences. They always decide everything who have nothing to do with anything. I think of the lost boy as a hamstrung falcon that was allowed to fly over no-man's land, but never beyond its own bounds. Yet Giovanni wasn't he beautiful! My first love. No woman had lips as soft as his. Nevertheless, we limited ourselves to that one kiss whose memory is my keepsake. I took Giovanni by the hand and led him to my friend Pietro Vanucci, the Vanucci from silent Perugia, for him to paint the beautiful boy. My women didn't understand. Now they keep the portrait in Florence, where it hangs like a secret crown in a corner of the Uffizi, so delicate and pale as nothing else in the world; and time and again I go there to kiss the boy's lips, at an unguarded moment, so their sweetness will rekindle the gift of life, for I am an aging man. . . .

Thusly the likes of us are consoled by the Mediterranean's great exhaustion—which is comprehensible, isn't it, given its weighty history. The young revolve around the old, satellites of a joint conspiracy called education, maturity, history; the young revolve in bright ellipses, parabolas, and sometimes hyperbolas. The hyperbolic line—that's what happened to Giovanni—does not return to its beginning.

Giovanni died young, but before that happened he was beautiful, was my child. It wasn't I who bestowed the common name Giovanni on him: he was born with it: as armor against callowness. The child was my son yet my lover. Human faces are imprecise, and human eyes see imprecisely. We stumble over new faces but not a one sates our hunger for a lasting order, a lasting construction. Giovanni was beautiful.

The precious color of imaginable eyes, the skin and tiny folds of possible lips, the precision of a dreamed creation—we find none of it. The man in the crowd has no eyes; he was created according to a law which does not exist. Rampant cells, following the animalistic principle of nature . . . And a man emerges who'd do well to hide his face. When people like that die no sound and no image is left behind. Nothing remains, they weren't unique but interchangeable . . . But then comes the day when the chosen one sees the *beautiful* person. The select flinches, he adjusts his soul to the utmost precision, he forgets all discretion and lays siege to the beautiful person. When everything, and thus nothing, of the beautiful person has been conquered, the face—after an audible click—is forever registered in the discoverer's soul. This click is love, and love is anguish: a collection of pores, a fluff, light angling iridescently into the iris.

If I'm digressing from the dead boy, then I'm also making my way to my aging mother, who's now slowly becoming unsure of herself. A great Spanish lady: she likes to stand at the window and look at the nearby cemetery. The view reminds her of something that struck her on one of her visits there. Softly, more to herself than to me, the mother says: the gravediggers heaped earth on the graves again today, yet there are cracks everywhere. She is speaking very softly. . .

Then she passes through the bedroom with its two large beds, one of which has stood empty since Father's death. She sighs before these vessels of sleep, and says, again to herself: yes, yes, even in the apartment everything's becoming more cramped . . . only the beds, only the beds keep growing . . .

Again I feel oppressed by the great embarrassment which made my home life so suffocating. I step to the bookshelf to take a book and leaf through it. How fragile Mother's becoming! She's scarcely ever been happy her whole life, nor was I able to do anything about that. I try to laugh. But with this woman, who's not really old and yet sometimes already far off, my shabby laughter fails. How to come closer to Mother, I ask myself, forgetting that Mother comes to me, spares me all effort as always. And I recall the big trip we took many years ago. Mother, do you remember our trip? Do you ever think about Lago di Bolsena, about the lovely eel, anguilla alla vernaccia, that we ate with such pleasure, the Montefiascone wine?

But Mother scrupulously tugs at the lace doily on the night table. She is not listening. She mumbles, to be sure, "I remember. . . ." yet I sense how she's thinking about other things, about darker, more immediate things. I leave the room and would like to weep. What a blessing it is when sons die before their mothers. After all, mothers are used to suffering. They're on good terms with birth and death. But sons can't endure much, especially not the death of their mothers. . .

* * *

The child has drained the bottle. Now it's screaming again. It is still thirsty.

CHAPTER VIII

Why We Are No Longer Worthy of the Plague

The Danube. When you finally manage to get free of the waltzing river, you arrive at the point where your eyes espy a distant light; but then you realize that a dark stream is flowing between you and the light, and that it is flowing even though it seems motionless. Fog in midsummer, for it is July, almost August, when you sit at the shore, in Belgrade trying to fend off the mosquitoes. These gnats would love to chew up your words. But you fight for your nocturnal prayers, for the incredibly distinct stars with their forgotten names. After running a long time, you finally understand that the only thing that matters is motionlessness, silence, the mosquitoes, and the distant light. An animal cries out on the other side: the divided Germany which, so you've been told, was once undivided Germany. But you don't believe it. You only believe in its guilt. Wherever human dignity is betrayed, geography, language, and events take their revenge. When, after what has happened, a work by Johann Sebastian Bach or Mozart is performed, you can't help your conviction that such music no longer belongs to the culprits. They have forfeited their right to it. Yet while the people in the East suffer, the people in the West choke on their lack of scruples. But the sufferers have been cleansed of the common guilt whereas the West's guilt increases, becoming less and less redeemable with every laugh. Thus the poor fellows' language exhausts itself in a bit of mad lamenting, in a little bit of begging—so as to win themselves a respite, which only deepens the despair.

How many pictures of peace, how many pictures of dying, how many pictures of battle my friend in Auvers-sur-Oise has painted! He painted his self-portraits for one purpose only: to enforce encounters, to be able to escape his solitude for a moment. Now I can see that the East and the West could use a self-portrait, that the olive trees created in Saint-Rémy are corpses risen from the grave. Furious, not sleepy. Auschwitz on Judgment Day, that's what these trees are . . . and the chair and the candle become more glaring, brighter, purer. The books become purer since no one wants to read them any more.

* * *

When I finally awoke to the new day, alone, in Siena, in a single room, I cast regret and jealousy aside. Man can find beauty only by himself, a ghost finds itself in like manner. I wrapped myself in a literary mood, paid my bill and traveled on. I drove by myself to Paris and hoped to find calm on this journey. All roads lead back to Siena; the possible detour, only that, can become our small freedom. Whoever possesses Europe as I, Don Juan, do, will scrape up a few extra miles before the

Siena road sign shows up again. A master at exchanging tiresome people, I found myself unexpectedly alone again, was not I, but my legend.

* * *

While crossing the Seine such hordes of people streamed toward him that he could hardly take two steps in succession. It was evening, and he was on his way on the narrow foot bridge to the Tuileries Gardens, whereas the masses were making for the suburban stations of the Rive Gauche. Wherever he looked, he saw rushing pedestrians, and indeed he was the only person on the bridge on his way to the gardens. So he fought his way through the crowd, sickened by the contact to which he was subjected there. As if seeking help, he glanced down at the filthy brown Seine and, fortified by the river, those walking into him no longer bothered him. Even the water remained water, for all its filth. Almost lovingly he regarded the suicides' favorite watery goal as it flowed westward, and, pacing easily, he reached the right bank.

The distance between the garden statues kept growing from death to death. Don Juan measured the world not in steps, not in despair, but in the unarticulated syllables of the question: in what direction progress would take its terrible growth? Necessary future space was only to be won, if at all, by casting humanity brutally aside, yet: this re-won space could not accommodate man's loss. Perhaps as a playground for future monsters the gardens had been assigned ultimate dimensions whose limits were in evidence, even now, everywhere. Don Juan did not linger long under the pallid trees of the night and of his unadorned thoughts, but began to walk ever more hastily out to the Rue de Rivoli. He crossed it awkwardly and, passing the Place Vendôme, passing the house in which Chopin had died, reached his beloved Café de la Paix.

There he withdrew into a corner in the back room, to think of various matters, including Chopin. In former times he had had quiet talks with the slender creature who suffered the curse of being unreal, had quiet talks that could prove very useful to the world, which cannot appreciate Chopin. But the talks went the way of the wind.

Don Juan was already reveling again in the sweet memories that distanced him from dying, and lost himself in the world to which he clung ever more passionately each day, as though the world were real. Neither Don Juan nor Chopin can move the world, since compassion always remains infinitesimally small, because there is no such thing as compassion.

Chopin was a frail Don Juan. Both Don Juan and Chopin glowed with the same innocence, but the Pole's skin was more delicate, and his demon denied him lust. Chopin was a man of dangerous intelligence, who was annihilated by his own heart. Don Juan liked wandering over to the Père Lachaise. On such afternoons at the cemetery he became adroit at locating graves, finally became expert, even at night, at finding the new addresses of Oscar Wilde, of Honoré de Balzac, of the pale

Chopin, whose graves Don Juan studied with the same cold-bloodedness with which Chopin had calculated his romanticism. Of all things *his* grave had to be of soft marble! amidst all that decay, and the visitor discovered dreaminess where its opposite rested: anguish. If a Don Juan and a Chopin had jointly settled for the truth, then the lie of art would have shattered before them. But, as it was, they too partook of the lie, concealed their true faces, and so were idealized; people saw radiance where there was the wetness of tears.

How glad the deaf ladies in this gilt Café de la Paix would have been to have a Steinway & Sons grand in the middle of the room; how gladly they would have seen a virtuoso in front of the piano, a dumb master of the keyboard, of superfluous décor, so they could hear their, the bad Chopin, who had nothing in common with his message. Don Juan, in his corner, could have supplied much that was mathematical, but he kept silent. Because certain ladies chose to fall in love with tall, slim pianists, because they instantly turn the dumb and the brown-eyed into a suffering prince, striplings into angels, the world takes no interest in Chopin.

But Don Juan was a fragment of Chopin, just as he was a fragment of the Café de la Paix; and a fragment of our indifference. Thus he would have been the link we all seek, but he preferred to remain a guest only. The old waitress with the lace apron set an éclair on the plate in front of Don Juan, and the Spaniard relished his nearness to death, which liqueurs and tarts sweetened for him. His silence could have finality, because Chopin's music was final.

Yet music had meant little to the Pole; his ideas mattered much more to him than the piano allowed him to work out. We clutch at every straw when we have something to say that is threatened by silence. Chopin's music scarcely justifies the concept of composition: his works are short, elegiac, and, above all, laden with adjectives, since we alone provide this contents, since we do not know why Chopin wrote his works. His music occasionally sounds hollow, because it must soar in order not to lose its affinity to our heaviness. Wherever supreme intelligence seeks expression, we immediately suspect godly artistry; wherever a pathology of the spirit suddenly manifests itself, we are blinded by a revelation.

The fear of being buried alive: that is one key to his music. We translate the anxieties in the mind into paralysis of the body, or demand to have our heart stabbed posthumously so that our work won't vanish. The *Etudes* rate highest, their very name reconciles. The *Scherzi* are mostly a deadly jest; *Nocturnes* are made of nighttime tears and morning dew; the *Ballads*—a pathetic swindle; *Mazurkas*: nostalgia ought to be private; *Waltzes* and Don Juan: one virgin per dedication . . . What remains important is the brain impulse which sometimes draws up a pact with the soul, thus becomes a link again.

Finally, the beauty in this music is confusing, because its sensuality flutters; heightens, because it resounds, without a kick. Chopin was human too, that alone makes him unapproachable. Only his grave is easy to reach: past that aging child, Cherubini, who is his playmate at night. For the more deeply we must suffer, the more important playing becomes, and what more is art if not playing? It would be ludicrous if Chopin and this little Cherubini, if these two played four-handed, which is why we would tremble with awe.

Contradictions even in mathematics, and no recourse to logic. Only the café provides a place of calm; the confectioner is the judge of God and of Chopin. Music of the spheres is not music, but a fine howling on a summer day which, barbarically, is akin to the super-sonic dog whistle. At such a sound heaven slip-faults earthward, the earth soars up to heaven. The summary crackling of high-tension wires sometimes has a grasp on this miracle: the future is creating its cheap and banal music of the spheres, which howls through heaven while God incarnate rots away.

* * *

Don Juan's unworldly manner excluded the reading of newspapers. But just now he happened to be leafing through a journal that lay on the table, glanced at the headlines, if that, yet was instantly outraged at the trash he found there. No, that's not what the day looked like. In the journal of Don Juan's opinion, the lead articles of that day would scarcely have made the back page; when he ran across a brief piece with the word "plague" in its title. Recalling his flight from plague-ridden Siena, Don Juan read these lines to the end. Several people in an African nation had become infected with the Bubonic Plague; the World Health Organization had been alerted. At the same time, the piece stressed that modern medicine knew how to prevent the spread of this once deadly disease of the Middle Ages.

Don Juan, whose life was also made difficult and painful because the words "earlier" and "later" were inconceivable—the universe being something timeless and immediate for him—smiled grimly at the journalistic nonsense—he should not even have touched the paper, he still made the stupidest mistakes.

As far as he was concerned these lines were lacking the horror, but also the glory and the mysticism which the plague deserved. In those days, 1348 A.D., when the Black Death did not so much crawl as race through the narrow alleys of Europe, of Siena, when it held its St Vitus' Dance, Don Juan had noticed at once that it had transformed people and, from the artist's point of view, had improved them. The oldest and grayest mice suddenly flashed by in the most varied colors: mad fear and deathly sweat polished the man in the street into a stone of rare beauty. Don Juan had a frontrow seat at the premiere, the plague had become his great danger but also his wild beloved. No one knew the director of the plague, but Don Juan guessed right that it couldn't be God. The direction was too masterful for that. Lucifer too, who after all was only a fallen angel, lacked the right keyboard for the plague. Don Juan had fallen in love with the director . . . The meanest crime did not lack in a seductive element, and the most animalistic fear of death produced the most splendid street scenes.

This was the first flowering of Baroque Theater, anticipated by some three hundred years; a stroke of genius by the director when mad-sense devoured wooden sense. Oh those the years of the Black Plague, the Middle Ages at their apogee which ended in a mad crash, and the Renaissance opening its night-blossoms whose scent is with us to this day. The keening and praying of the dying added to the broad wide background noises of the colossal play which no world war or tragedy would later duplicate. Whoever became used to the plague would scarcely notice this deathly roar, just as we—consciously yet unwitting—draw the lapping ocean waves into our sleep on the shores.

Nakedly and alluringly rattling fear danced while death celebrated his wild premieres and lewd reprise on the steepest grades. Men carrying the deadly disease raped virgins and children under the universal cover of panic. The men's panting formed a horrible union with the children's impotent screams. In the esthetic absence of feeling and of law, forced sexual intercourse received death's blessing. For it was ludicrously pedantic to weep for lost innocence or for the anguish that the promise of the painful lust of being penetrated produced, because it was not merely the seed of animalistic men but the seed of death that began to widen each defile.

That was the plague: a burning of the deathbeds, though only a few made it home to their beds, perishing instead on the cobblestones of the alleys. A thousandfold funeral pyre from north to south: that was the plague, that big, and Don Juan, who had always misused death as lust's companion, had emerged alive from these horrors, a hellish heavenly Phoenix that, not risen, flew downward, screwing into human filth, human meanness, and who finally reached the clarity of the burning depths. Don Juan had made it this far, to the Café de la Paix, where suddenly another survival became decisive. So he had left Siena a second time, leaving his blind companion behind. In old age, Don Juan found a chemical formula for indifference, which had replaced the plague. Indifference was the heiress to Queen Plague who only despises us. This drew Don Juan away from the real world into the stage set world of music where Queen Plague sang her fallow coloraturas.

CHAPTER IX

Night at the Opera.

If Don Juan had divided his life into recitatives and arias, if he had been able to anticipate a Mozart and had had the opportunity to insinuate the damnation of Don Juan into Mozart's quill, he would still have been disappointed. No changing of facts could mitigate the truth that Don Juan had coursed through the centuries anything but harmoniously, and that he himself was to blame for having led mankind by the nose. The artistic misunderstandings that flared up like summer lightning all around Don Juan only to fade away again were the context of the insistent blundering by a great personality, blunders which the Spaniard had—if involuntarily—of course staged himself. Even if he had completed his unwritten memoirs in masterly Mozartian fashion, his life still would not have been a highpoint of literature, but an endless, failed monologue at best. Don Juan's life did not allow of much room for other voices: Leporello became superfluous; a variety of ladies did better to hold their plaintive tongues. The avenging commendatore, too, was a clown like all of those others who insisted on their own authority over and beyond anyone else's, and through whose fingers Don Juan slipped.

Don Juan did not appreciate the opera's shortcomings. Though Monteverdi had been his close acquaintance, the breach that Gluck introduced, only Mozart was able to reconcile it, one last time. But then the man from Salzburg wrote his *Don Giovanni*, this absolute masterpiece, which filled Don Juan with pride but also with understandable anger; which made him distance himself from the world of opera altogether. True, he continued to love the Avenue de l' Opéra, which even for the centuries-old man reeked with far too much allure for him not to keep walking it. He actually loved the ornate opera building though he described an anxious detour around its entrance. Nevertheless, the opera-near Café de la Paix remained his favorite haven; there he put down anchor when fatigued, and with aristocratic discipline took his modest spot in the back room. There he was safe from operatic airs of all kind, there no voluptuous evening gown would appear and make him restless.

For some time his only neighbor in that exile had been the ancient Duchess of S. who, since her husband's death, had decreed the Café her waiting room where—tired of her past—she was dozing into death. The Duchess always wore black, pearls her only décor but her truest jewel her silence, her inability to smile, a value she maintained until she no longer appeared. She, too, had always picked the hind most corner, so as to be safe from the street crowd brazenly staring through the windows. Initially we make demands of our death, saying: I won't go until such-and-such happens, but then we take our departure unconditionally, worn out by the wretched waiting.

To remain stubbornly blind to the opera takes tremendous resolve. But even this strength can be worn down, surreptitiously, by resignation, and soon our obstinacy has left us exhausted. Our eyelids begin to flutter once our proud NO comes to nought at the opera gates. Is it recitative or aria, which distortion fits the bankrupt nobleman best? For there was no staunching his bankruptcy; the inner fire didn't reach the melting point any more; he was losing his grip on his thoughts: he was contemplating All Souls' Day with too much passion to feel at ease in sunlight. Whoever's future is full of such dark intimations soon has his past for a coffin.

* * *

Oscar Wilde had the habit of sitting, not in the corner of the back room, but on the outside terrace. Even in his last worst days, when his suits went unbrushed and his wines *sans appellation*, the poet sat out on the terrace so that his presence would not miss anybody. Only someone who would die without having realized himself could still be so frenzied for life; and Don Juan, for whom the interval between then and now was no longer than a concert pause, felt sorry for this Mediterranean Irishman, who was turning corpulent, whose innocence of this world had discovered that delicate equation according to which beauty shied away from health and resided more comfortably in the perversions. That notable therory Don Juan, too, was prepared to endorse. Yet the two gentlemen never met, a regrettable circumstance, for they could have taught each other much. Don Juan could have afforded the mute poet new despair to help him write, and the dying Irishman's story would have told the Spaniard much about love. No matter how marvelous Wilde's life may have been, his miserable death can't help but disgust us. Mr. Wilde had deserved a better death. The burnt-out poet, the inspired chatterbox, who had been long dead for the public before he actually died, continued to live inside Don Juan. *Rigor mortis* does not set in so rapidly that all it takes is less than a century for you to be buried by such an ice age of indifference that a dead man can't stir a single heart. Mr. Wilde wrote a few beautiful stories which bring tears even to the heartless, he was enthusiastic about fairy tales from the Bible, which he adopted and embraced, not due to any kinship to the Biblical landscape, but due to his joy in childish pain.

Salome, the wild princess, he transformed into a playful child just discovering her own body. The murder of the saint is nothing but soft masturbation. Don Juan smiled about the fact that the music for this piece of voluptuousness comes from *Deutschland*, of course, once again confirming the subtle dictatorship of the devil, even if Richard Strauss did sign the score.

* * *

Having succumbed to the unknown magic, feeling kinship to lusting necrophilia, Don Juan rediscovered himself at the Opera. The house was shrilly packed, everything was brightly lighted, decorated and dressed, to celebrate the opera hater's return. The snapping eyes of the human fishes were directed shamelessly at him so that he was forced to show himself, to make shallow repartees, and allow gray recognition. But Don Juan was not alone. The girl from the distant summer festival hung light as a feather on his right arm. (Invisibly chained to his left, however, he of course carried the suitcase filled with details about the opera, about lust, and the law of the eternal return.)

Thus the Spaniard led the girl to the gallery whence they looked down the stairwell, at the thousands who pretended they had come to watch this *Salome*. If these guests of boredom had any comprehension of the opera's sensual luxuriations in icy coldness, youth's robust love of murder, they gave evidence of this only in the most childish fashion. The sage and the youthful girl leaned over the balustrade, both of them immune to vertigo—youth too callow and old age too indifferent to it. It was time to enter the hall.

As Don Juan settled into his velvet chair again, wearily certain of his own box, he recognized the hallucinated ceiling by Marc Chagall. Chagall is reputed to have said that he discovered Light the first time he stepped from the train in Paris. Alas! And in bizarre gratitude for this discovery, he had then painted this putrid scene that darkens the opera with its slashes of color. Gilded putti from another age stretched up painfully beneath this work, and the elegant chandelier lost its glow and the many-faceted play of its light. Don Juan despised this Opera House, but once he was seated in the the box, he began gently to love it as he loved everything that flowed.

* * *

Why did people go to the opera, why didn't they rather force operas to attend other operas, to be each other's guests? The envisioned goal would be an autarchy of operas, operas that no longer needed man. Macbeth should yawn at Othello, Sarastro tremble before Salome; Don Carlos would sing *Der Freischütz.* Just as chess pieces are limited to sixty-four squares, so the figures of opera should remain restricted to their operatic realm, never enter the outside world. If scores play for other scores, peace would finally be attained, that heavenly peace of which Don Juan had been dreaming for centuries.

But the hall was jammed with people, none of whom wanted to miss the entrance of the princess, the entrance of her shrill puberty in front of dolled-up voyeurs. St. Mark already reports the evil story, but the texts of saints are rarely artful, their sentences lack lust and blood. Mr. Wilde, on the other hand, was convincing, he accessed his own resources, feeling at one with his erroneous ways, and, besides, understood the purity of the saints.

Don Juan sat strangely excited in his loge. For ages he had sought to flirt with this princess, his boyish dreams had played with her hot body, but he had failed to reach his objective. The princess had denied him his lust, he had no luck with this stubborn child. Yet he leered for this doll of innocence and awakening sensuality. Why did Salome have to die before Don Juan had even been born, and why could he not find her skeleton anywhere, so as at least to kiss the bones where her lips might have been—after all, the princess received the cooling lips of Jochanaan in the light of day? Don Juan had finally found one being he could not undress because she, Salome—in disregard of him—had died before he was born. For the first time there was a lack of reality, which was why it became that much more enticing.

The Spaniard's thoughts began to drift as soon as the stagegirl-child failed to seduce Jochanaan, not because the saint's celibacy was all powerful, but because the princess's seductive maneuvers were still too inept. It would be too good to be true, Don Juan cogitated, if original sin really did exist, if church dogma were compatible with God's love, for if original sin did exist, then wretched humans wouldn't first have to go through such toil to acquire it—some bumblers can't even manage it before they die.

Jochanaan stands there on the stage: a ludicrous apparition, an ugly fool who fails to seize when beauty offers itself to him. The saint comes out looking an imbecile in front of the thousands of people in this Opera House; he disdains what he could never get on his own, because he is too rigid, too boring. Salome, however, is young and delicious; she dances around that hulk of innocence, who can barely save his precious skin, who smells sin and whose sacred naiveté knows not that youth is always innocent, that beauty forgives almost anything, and that one night of love between Jochanaan and that demanding child would engender a doubled innocence; that enjoyment is one way to the divine. But the hollow law of good and evil is not found in life alone; it also lies in the superstructure of the theater.

Don Juan feels like whispering into the girl's ear that sin can be sublime and majestic, that its movement lies in the middle, whereas the saint, like a village idiot, is still living in the cow sheds. But Don Juan keeps to himself and says nothing.

Then, when there's a suicide at the edge of the stage, when Narraboth falls, Salome and Jochanaan don't even look over at him. In their averted gaze they finally become as one; where compassion and looking are required, they are as blind as winter, are coupled in this blindness. For a *Liebestod*, the saint has nothing but his damnation, like heaven he hasn't a glance to spare for the dying man, nor does Salome bother, because Narraboth's death failed to heed her decree. It is the blindness of the self-righteous which consigns God and the Devil to be the amateurs of this earth, miserable, incompetent spirits.

But Jochanaan climbs back down into his dank cistern. He shrinks from the brilliant footlights, the barrenness of the end of the world is quite becoming for the steep career of a saint. Parisians or New Yorkers are not likely to become saints, but Thérèse of Lisieux, Jeanne d' Arc, or the country girl from Lourdes managed the leap into grace—the call of heaven remained unmistakable in their desolate villages.

Don Juan saw decadence as an actual withdrawing of your self into innermost rooms, as an urgent turning inward, and as the closing of many doors, until the stale air turns into foulness and incense. Decadence for him was the time of the advent of death, a silent drawing of shades, a darkening inside the head, and a sadness that gradually chokes us. Once Salome had her way, and Jochanaan's head lies on a silver platter, the girl's pubescent obstinacy melts in her first orgasm. Thighs half parted, Salome is lying on the stage, she kisses the bloody, luke warm, cold lips . . . pursues her sweet necrophilia, and during her kiss, *love* resounds from the orchestra. Love was written all over the handful of notes which embroider this horrendous kiss, but no one in the audience heard anything but sounds.

Don Juan was a literary man if only because perhaps he was not alive. Scarcely more than a symbol for most of us, he had disembodied himself masterfully, completely disappeared into literature, and yet he lived freed of literature, drawing more breaths of life than poor van Gogh whose traces are documented by history. Don Juan accused the opera of the misuse of power of its music, for music in its dishonest way was more reliable than language which deceives the reader no matter how possessed by the truth a writer may be when he sets his words. Music pretends to and creates an aura of togetherness, it needs no burden of proof. Whoever lives with words alone lives dreadfully alone, will always seem suspect. Don Juan could not expect credibility, he knew himself to be fragilely suspect. For her part, night after night, somewhere in the world, Salome has her dance: and in the last act kisses the chill lips, is reincarnated on a stage and receives fresh applause. And yet she is no figure for the stage, is not a Biblical whore and not a princess but—chiefly—just a girl: a human being, whereas Don Juan is nothing but a literary man and literature.

But before that curse had time to sink in, Don Juan had already become hopelessly old. Aging does not mean much, death rarely obeys the laws of time, but to be increasingly anxious is a sure sign. Lost in the music again, Don Juan clasped his guest's hand, which started up at the pressure of his bony fingers. Much too loud, with no regard for the audience, he formed sentences which yesterday he would have denied himself.

I'm afraid of memories, I'm afraid of the present. I'm afraid of my life and I'm afraid of death. I would have left a long time ago if I weren't afraid of taking the step. This fear is the drumbeat of my failure. The inner clock and the outer clock can be wrong, can miscalculate, but fear never miscalculates. Twice I've escaped the plague; never will I escape my fear.

God must know that I believe in him, that I'm nesting like a termite in Cimabue's destroyed cross, quietly and full of humility. God must know that I'm not his enemy, but that I merely articulate mankind's doubts somewhat more loudly than our weakness normally permits. He must know that I, the great seducer of mankind, rub mankind's weakness only somewhat more naughtily under his nose, so that He won't overlook our lack of backbone. I don't want to be overlooked any more, yet am only a ghost. How painful it must be for mankind once no God takes notice of them.

—Miss, I want to go home to Seville, to rest on a wooden bench in my first tavern, in the *Hosteria del Laurel,* until some heaven will grow over my death-bed.

—Don't look at me, Miss, please look at the stage, where the underpaid extras move around so believably, so perfectly. People of the lowest, most wretched classes which they are almost without exception, these extras play their parts best of all. Of course they have the easiest roles, they never have to open their mouths, their hurriedly made-up faces are too far from the boxes to disappoint the audience. These extras know to take perfect bows. For their audience they act out an astonishing display of respect and politeness that is out of fashion outside the theater. Nor was such politeness ever customary, I think, among creatures of their position. The extras are trained to play for the audience what they are not. This way of *seeming* all by itself has something consoling about it.

—Today, after a hundred years without theater, after these years during which I was alienated and indifferent to stars and extras alike, I enjoy this opera again. After all, no matter the play, no matter that invariably wrongheaded theme, no matter who the author, what counts is the magic of the theater, the ghostly flitting of costumes and bodies. In Salome's dance of veils, I recognize the reality in which I do not participate. Excluded from the freshness of youth, I will always be oddly moved how couples manage to find each other on stage, how everything fits, how everything is so magically accommodated.

—The young admire the actors' stardom even if they detest the theater. Miss, all I need do is take one look into your eyes to see how sincere you are. You can stay awake for days and nights, without sleep, without ablution, mercilessly expose your feelings, and you still remain beautiful. Your freshness, Miss, lets me realize that I myself am an extra or a star, a theatrical being: sufferable only when well rested, when illuminated, when made up.

—Please look at this stage. For centuries I've known that theater is overwrought, more candid than reality. Novices' eyes pop when they enter the theater, they want to see everything. But the connoisseur closes his eyes. We must only learn to close our eyes; that's the key to the enjoyment of art.

—When I see these extras taking their bows, I suddenly think of the plague again. For you, Miss, Siena is only a word; even if you've been there, Siena remains only a word. Perhaps you know the city, yet you only know it physically. The exaltation of the plague will remain alien to you. "Thank God," you might want to reply, but you're mistaken; there's a kind of beauty that remains inaccessible to the people of our century; the multicolored plague is of that kind. Especially northern people have no hope ever of being worthy again of the plague. We're stuck in the swamp of mediocrity, we are no longer masters of the rules of staging the plague. Miss, I at least have broken my habit of thinking of the plague as a disease; I think of it as a play which no one may dare stage any more. Our society lacks the talent to provide the director for the new plague. We die without character, of cancer. The plague slumbers in the archives, no one has an idea of its importance for the stage. We should interrupt the performance here and protest, we should demand the plague on our stages, perhaps there'd be some hope then.

—Yet no one understands the plague's *goodness.* When it kills: extras, whole peoples; if the plague becomes the celebrated star, when it takes its bow before victims: "Wasn't that ever a brilliant performance?", then it becomes a loving mother taking our death—which we conduct bureaucratically, without talent—into her gentle hands. With its deathblow, the plague rouses its victims to real life, to theatricality. The dead, Miss, rediscover themselves.

—The theater is a noisy affair; its pathos is uncouth, until the pathos finally melts into hurting eyes and sweet intoxication. These are heady evenings, Miss, when love becomes a letting go, a stripping away of all dignity. There are men of the highest calling, true princes of the mind and heart who unwittingly diminish their fellow men, intimidate them, as a witch does a child. Others are just as great—and their presence raises human beings up to their level. The plague, too, leads to a brighter plain. . .

—Beyond that, I doubt whether any elevation or lowering of people is really possible. Our vague words convey a bit of courage, encouraging only those who have it in them to be so touched. . .

—. . . This sweet piece of necrophilia, whispered Don Juan, kissing his own hand, which was as cold as Jochanaan's lips.

CHAPTER X

Umbrian Fatigue

Having proved himself, throughout the centuries, one of the keenest readers of literatures which invariably called themselves modern, Don Juan finally grew weary of the tidal wave of new works. At first he hardly felt his curiosity waning, felt this only in company when five-day-wonder poets were discussed. Then he had to admit that not even their most accomplished works interested him. In the first phase of this fatigue it happened his flagging interest disconcerted him: and he would rush straight to book stores and buy works he would never read. The transition to indifference of course is not abrupt—like all diseases it takes its time. But such a development seems to suggest a downward trend and the so afflicted suffer, search everywhere for reasons, and frequently perish. Don Juan, too, acknowledged his growing tiredness as a further stage toward death.

Of course, the skillful littérateur was afforded detours, say into acid haughtiness and into cutting irony. A wordsmith might convince himself, and others, that he avoided books because their intellectual vacuousness was beneath his attention. All you need do was cut someone to shreds to feel like a big shredder! Journalists made a living doing this. But Don Juan no longer needed to fence with stupidity and irony. Though formerly public opinion had also mattered to him, we do not grow old for nothing.

For over a century now, the Spaniard had not frequented the gossipy rounds of the littérateurs. He had still visited Madame de Sevigné's parlor sporadically, but there had mostly kept silent. On such evenings, he had quietly sat by the fireplace and made observations of which his direct way of being had kept him from making notes. The French language, seasoned with Latin, had refreshed the Spaniard all his life: he liked to live with the sound of this language; he found in it the fluency lacking in his mother tongue. In these Parisian drawing-rooms he felt a connection to that intimate mysticism the origin of whose long, stringy roots was as distant as Germany and Russia.

Thus his favorite Parisian friends had been immigrants, and Chopin and poor Vincent were not the only ones in that electrically charged dead circle to whom Don Juan gave his loyalty. It is of the nature of literature to report the significant; that is, to make even the least important thing significant, and that is the only reason why these are major names. But the selection of course remains unjust, since injustice is another of art's building blocks.

Countless hollow names crossed Don Juan's path only to be uplifted from their supine positions, used for a night's pleasure, or for a few weeks' melodrama. Almost all of these names suffered, and cringed, because they could not comprehend why they were sacrificed. So the many thousand girls only felt the autumn, and the loneliness of the afterwards, and did not wear the seal of their proud relationship with a queen's dignity. So the pages and boys merely felt shamefully abused, without keeping these few hours' pleasure as a beacon for the rest of their life, this life in the filth of wives, of daily work, of baseness. It was Don Juan's destiny to bring dignity to men, and to release them, without pathos, from their dull lot. He too was a redeemer, immortal and destined for death. Thus Don Juan had traveled through Europe, the continents of the earth, and everywhere had heralded pleasure—because no one believed in it. Society banned Don Juan while secretly and hypocritically duplicating his callowness. So as not to have to look at themselves in the mirror, people called Don Juan an allegory, displacing him from the structure of nerve cells to the vacuum of the brain. But occasionally they allowed themselves an evening at the opera with him and then condemned him to hell. Don Juan read his name almost everywhere: on billboards, in bookstores, on opera playbills and in the bookshelves of libraries, and on dustjackets of all kinds; and this his manifold appearance filled him more with anger than pride. Even his eyesight was gradually failing, and when he went out for a breath of air, he hardly looked at bulletin boards, avoided the chaos in the shops, but looked for beautiful faces: a rare festive discovery.

* * *

He was sitting in the back room of the Café de la Paix and remembered his first trip to *Assisi.* Until it became dark he had stood on that terrace adjoining the saint's highest church and had gazed at the broad loving country of San Francesco. Even at that time, Europeans were fascinated by Don Juan's evil seductive reputation. But Don Juan had stood on the silent hill and wept. Since that night it had become his most secret wish to be a Franciscan monk and to live in the Assisi cloister in the utmost poverty and beauty. He told no one of his ambition, he only praised Umbria where man's and godly measures became one.

Giovanni, too, his son and lover, had come into the world here. A search for the unforgotten inscription, Via XIV Settembre, and a visit with his most beloved were out of the question of course—death had intervened once again, and Don Juan was once again ashamed of the timelessness of his existence; yet he knew that Assisi would outlast him, too. These monks in their rough cowls, whether they were young or old, spoke more fluently about eternity, and had a more severe experience of the fact than the Spaniard that human duration is not so much measurable in time as in a yea-saying to love.

Then there was the other *Giovanni,* metamorphosed like a butterfly, become a saint. Don Juan had loved the vain Giovanni Bernardone, who suddenly and modestly called himself *Francesco.* The seducer and he had had the same childhood, what difference is there if a boy spends his years in Andalusia or in Assisi? The silence of olive trees prevailed in the gardens of both boys; on the tables of both families, wine was part of the daily bread. The conditions of growing up loved were met in both houses; their beginnings were fraternally similar, but Umbria is blessed. Nowhere else in this world are the faces so knowing; nowhere else do such children flourish.

Don Juan took his solitary path, and Francesco chose his. Just as the saint made friends, men who joined him in donning the cowl of simple love, so the Spaniard established his congregation, that of the loosely uniformed who cast the fire of pure lust into the flame of Assisi's silence. Yet only their armies engaged in battle; the generals lived in fraternal closeness. Francesco had been Don Juan, had only taken an option on Don Juan's life but then dropped it, whereas Don Juan was still to become Francesco. The field marshals loved one another, only their armies hated, despised and served in that war which found its redemption in *Gubbio.*

The threesome had left the unique city and, passing through hidden turns and woods, through fog and somber clouds, had arrived at *Monte Sant' Ubaldo.* Though the wolf of Gubbio had not crossed their path, they were pursued by stray barking dogs for a stretch and this frightened Don Juan. On his Andalusian estates he of course had owned a large pack of hunting dogs who had been accorded the best of care, especially those of Moorish ancestry; but actually Don Juan had always been afraid of dogs. The tame animals terrified him more than the wild ones, elicited an aboriginal terror because Don Juan did not trust their pretext of tameness—he was always lying in wait for the outbreak of their true nature, a hidden viciousness which lay more or less dormant in these artificial creatures as well as in man. The semblance of an orderly day filled him with uncertainty and impatience. Then, close to the inn, the raging dogs had suddenly become friendly companions, dozing like cats beside the fireplace as soon as the wanderers entered the inn.

Don Juan's companions were a young boy and girl, brother and sister, whose faces and lips had Umbria written all over them, and Don Juan's affections were torn between them. Their conversation during their hike, which had become stormy because of their fear of the dogs and awe at the clouds, now fell silent in the smoky room where a sluggish proprietress set *prosciutto di montagna* and unsalted bread on the table. That incomparable view of the summer days, that of the wavelike monotony of Umbrian perfection on the opposite hillsides, was not on display for their eyes today. November, the month of scorpions, had erected cloud-banks, had dabbled around with the fog, and today, on Don Juan's birthday, the world looked nailed tight.

Don Juan's disappointed gaze drew its pleasure from the beauty of his young companions. Sundered by his desire for the girl and his longing for the boy, the old Spaniard muffled himself up in greenish gray. His face became a big olive that, shriveled yet widened by exposure to the summer heat, now looked in the direction of winter.

The two youngsters had no idea who was sitting opposite from them. In Gubbio people live without lies. They did not take the old fellow especially seriously but were prepared for a lighthearted adventure. Youth wants to be seduced, old age wishes to do so: thus creation comes full circle once again. Youth and old age, which cannot stand each other, need each other for vanity's sake. The dreams of youth are fundamentally pure, as they are fundamentally obscene, and thus youth becomes the place of reconciliation. The topsy-turvy of advancing years brings a cooling off, and only our monks and priests know how to love our youth, love them even sensually, since spiritual love alone cannot save mankind. It is the touching of hands and the fusion of helpless bodies that give form and color to the transparency of souls. Where there isn't lust to overflow unto a god, the promised heaven tastes stale.

Don Juan, who noticed the two near-children's appetite, gave up his share of the ham while mutely settling back into the delight of watching them. So long as he had youth around him the fog might envelop the inn forever. Don Juan would celebrate his birthdays and continue to add to his tab.

The two beauties sat in front of him, their skin flushed, eating, and waiting for the seduction. They would have tolerated embraces; they didn't know who the old man was. Don Juan undressed them in his mind, imagined how they would surrender themselves to him, but he knew of the need for restraint, of a patriarch's household duties. His strength had become limited, scarcely sufficed for chewing the ham, and he could not have the two, their youth was too sacred.

He ordered more bread and, by himself, went over to the church in which Sant' Ubaldo sleeps. *Sleeping* was the only word that did not fill the nobleman with fear. Death was as horrendous as the baying of hounds whence no one could decipher whether they were rabid or healthy. Yet another undecomposed saint slept here, another bishop in opulent vestments, he too a silent herald of peace who was preserving the impudent church's significance for it. Don Juan circled the coffin, this glassy cage of mercy, which he was not allowed to show the youngsters. Where old men find peace, children are all too quickly terrified, and have nightmares of fleshless corpses with wrinkled skin and miters. But he loved Sant' Ubaldo, loved the hope of not decaying, and the glassy calm with dogs barking in the fog outside.

His grave, the Spaniard knew, when his worthless name was mentioned, his grave would be libretti, trashy novels, and a shrugging of the shoulders. His saintliness remained to be attained, even though it did not stand open to the good man. Saintliness was not an overweening ambition, was not comparable to the highest attainable station, could just descend unconditionally on anyone. Grace was a lottery.

No one, not even he, seemed allowed to tarry here, and it was better to make for the door, to turn away from Sant' Ubaldo, and to step wearily. Don Juan did not want to disturb the silence of these monks; he would do better to return to brother and sister, whose expectations he no longer felt it was in his power to fulfill. Nights of love are youth's best and wisest game, every moment is for pleasure, and yet they would remain pure so long as beauty lived with beauty. Physical beauty far surpasses spiritual beauty, is far superior to goodness and has no path to the soul.

Don Juan sat down between the two again and did not touch them, merely studying their presence. He was glad that the Urbino angel, "*Raffaele* of the Hither Hills," was not the only perfect one here (Don Juan and *Santi* had valued each other). This boy, in this inn, was almost like the boy Santi: time at least does not threaten the standard of ultimate perfection. The man who must thwart his becoming wholly human, man's expectations, knowledge, and trust, and discovery of his limits over the years, that man could be certain yet of one constant: that beauty does not lessen, that it changes the form it takes but only conditionally, and that even tomorrow there will be born someone who will preserve perfection.

Though her noble face ill-suited her rustic name, Annalisa, the sister, bore it negligently. What counted was that she knew how to laugh without abandoning her melancholy, which is a prerequisite for masterfulness of any kind. Don Juan was tempted to tell the children no end of stories but he kept his words to himself. He was not a born teacher; he suffered his chains alone.

He let tears be his instructors; the right to administer examinations belonged to heavy melancholy. He did not believe in the force of avalanches; he despised the merely seeming severity which is on winter's side.

A farmer took them back to the city in his Fiat. Don Juan feigned indifference, but the drive came just in time, for he felt in pain, yet another pain. If you are ill and are suffering, no philosophy is of use, and even beauty leaves the scene. Disappointed but reassured, the two children said their good-byes to the old man, went rushing down the narrow street, and shouted a last *ciao* up to him from below before turning the corner, the frontier post of his solitude.

* * *

The exhausted man ordered his evening meal in a simple trattoria he had never been in before. The pains concentrated in his back, whence they trickled down into his hips, to take up night quarters finally in his legs. The arches of this inn had aged together with Don Juan: and what a long journey it had been. The ceiling was brittle and damp, the air was of a peculiar frostiness. That was the disadvantage of old buildings, of reminding their inhabitants too much of the grave; the resemblance to tombs was too conspicuous, not subtle enough for the living, too glaring as a reminder for those already close to death. Don Juan had lived eye to eye with beauty for an afternoon, had rashly climbed the mountain with the youngsters, had tossed all care to the winds and, despite it all, now sat alone by himself plagued by pains and in expectation of tortellini, which were not quite the same either anymore, yet another of this century's adulterations.

The proprietress was dribbling trivia while she brought the steaming bowl and filled the guest's plate, and Don Juan was forced to respond if he did not want to be impolite, and the proprietress immediately stumbled over the foreign, primally Spanish undertone that gurgled in his Italian, and expressed her amazement: such an old man, and still traveling! . . . Then she praised his Italian, the accent was of no account. Don Juan swallowed hard—even his eight hundred years' practice speaking the alien tongue had not made it his own; even now he was still just borrowing words.

The innkeeper disappeared in the kitchen, Don Juan ate his meal making loud smacking sounds. His behavior was becoming coarser, and occasionally he forgot his upbringing altogether, not that it had ever stood him in much stead; it had only burdened him with complexes that jangled inside him as if he were a drum full of old tin cans. His life's great achievements, which had earned him fame and outrage, were born of impudent disregard of all the rules and were not the legacy of the best upbringing his class afforded him. He was the only guest at the inn; more and more frequently the only guest and wondered what had happened to the rest of the world.

He also dropped the last vestiges of his comic play-acting; pains his only audience, they did not applaud the artist. His mistakes only hurt him now, he had become a harmless ancient. Even love, which he had sought steadfastly to the end, Don Juan now tossed to the winds; old men suspect that they are being ridiculed when someone seeks out their hands.

The only thing he continued to be afraid of was dying. Sometimes, between soup and roast, this fear flared up, and killed his hunger. Then, soup-spattered, he returned to his senses and forced himself to shut up; though, like an infant, he wanted nothing as much as to bawl: no, not death, I'm afraid of dying! Once he had composed his thoughts again, he came up with a bit of sophistry to explain his undignified panic attacks: he, Don Juan, must not die so long as Europe had not died; he must remain in Umbria; who besides him cared for it so deeply? Who besides him had heard Vincent's confession; who besides him had possessed the positively metaphysical bodies of one thousand and three Spanish girls and women? Whoever commandeth Don Juan's wealth of experience must not die; the world ought to reach out for him, should strive to hold him, for if he went, then the great harmonious cycle would be extinguished with him. And yet, if he died in the here and now of this cheap inn, only the proprietress would know, would grouch about his tab, perhaps fleece his pockets; then, unmoved, wait for new guests, one guest as good as the other. How many innkeepers made up this world?

Now his stomach, too, began to ache; perhaps he'd even been poisoned. Of course the nobleman's fears ill-suited the grief-sicken sage. He brooded himself into a ruined evening that was not part of the bright afternoon that this day had granted him. But how was he to think brightly when only a single lamp cast its light here, a sparse energy saving device at that, an insult to Don Juan, who had seen tens of thousands of candles in one of the *Palacio Real's* halls? Formerly he would never have guessed that life in this century could lead to the inconceivable poverty that was now the parquet of his and everyone's daily life.

Despite his surfeit of disgust, he did not want to die! A Spanish aristocrat who had remained a gentleman, even in the rubble of our octopus-like democracies, could not accept becoming a plaything of death. His close friend Henry de Montherlant, that last literary aristocrat, who had recently died, was to be his model. The solitary monsieur of the Quai Voltaire had not wished to be a plaything either, so he denigrated death into a plaything, proving to the bourgeois Hamlets that nothing should belittle the resolve to have done with it as long as there is still a strong will. Toys like pistol barrels in the mouth, like that all-powerful weakling Death who, dancing everywhere, fails to challenge his partner and commits his murder most foully from behind. The bright-coated skeletons that dangle from the stained-glass windows of Lübeck's Marienkirche stir anxiety in some observers; in others they have not stirred anything for a long time. The *danse macabre* of his childhood had been only a game with leaded window panes, the church's sly falsification of the balance sheet to teach old women to tremble with fear: for every nightmare two farthings more tithe; for every confession two cups of wine.

Don Juan had long since seen through that con game, and had been hit with a papal letter of excommunication, the Papal Bull of unlovingness. The letter with the papal seal lay gathering dust in the Spanish castle, but perhaps Don Juan's prayers in Umbrian churches had reached heaven. At any event, they added to the land's ripeness, ruffling the westerly clouds at nightfall. But there was a suicide in Don Juan's future: how else are immortals to die: a voluntary death—what a nice phrase. For if someone lives for many centuries, he loses his belief in violence. The journey toward Charon becomes an adventure. But how awful it would be if this taking leave only half succeeded, if they found him and detained him, herding him into the nets of life, if the world press documented his legendary existence: reporters storming to his hospital bedside, doctors transfusing the blood of plebes?. . . A man of Don Juan's infirmity was no longer sure of success, feared the insidious tricks his body played, the endlessly twitching heart. He knew his antagonist was the un-mind.

He had no friends left to help him make his journey easier, to obtain for him the most appropriate poison which, three hundred years ago, he had put in his signet ring. The ring had long since disappeared; objects had a centrifugal quality which was out of tune with the harmony of belonging, away from warmth of protective hands, out into absolute coldness. His poison had crumbled long ago, all he had left was the illusion of a will that, like a puberty-stricken adolescent, bellows for death.

Now he asked for his bill and paid it with the accustomed generosity that had so impressed his friends at—Doctor Faustus still a child—Auerbach's cellar. The proprietress was an old woman; only her heirs would benefit by the tip, but she glowed nevertheless. Money made people happy, even the dying grasp for it. Two old people were standing in the room, one of them grasping, the other making ready to leave, the two barely one step apart yet lacking any warmth and closeness, not the least complicity flourishing between them. Don Juan knew that this woman would be the last person he would see alive. Thus leave-taking of humanity was hideous, devoid of beauty, of mourning, was a filthy gesture, a grab. Perhaps Don Juan, who had craved and possessed women with such passion, should have clasped the old woman's hand, but he knew the hand would be cold as Jochanaan's lips, and Don Juan shied away from the dead.

It had become colder in Gubbio; the assurance of the south lost all claims to certainty. The Spaniard walked down the same street that the children had taken earlier. They were now asleep behind one of the dark windows, or were dreaming. Perhaps their young ears would pick up the slurping step of his heavy feet on the perceptive ground, but no sleeper asks about the night wanderer; the sleeper hears and dozes off again, deeper into nightly absence. Noise resounded from a tavern. Don Juan hid in the shadows and then scurried along the walls of the houses out of town. The thick belt of the city-wall closed before him, but day and night were indistinguishable now, the gates had long since been torn from their hinges, the fugitive saw his flight abetted.

Out here he suddenly felt the wind that was driving the clouds toward the Adriatic like pauper's rags, like corpses' veils. In their midst there stood, rarely enough, some stars, like birthday candles for Don Juan. He reached up with his arms, drawing down the mellowest one. Then he reached his car which, out of exaggerated consideration for this precious city, he had parked outside the city walls, beside the old cistern that perhaps held the good saint and which perhaps surrounded evil physics with some goodness. Don Juan felt thirsty, but once before someone had asked for water and had only received vinegar. So he tamed his thirst and unlocked the car door.

He wanted to put Umbria behind him, to pass through childishly shy Urbino and, this very night, to reach the sea. The narrow Adriatic Sea would have to suffice for his thoughts which were yearning for the ocean, for arrival, and for bathing at gray daybreak, for ultimate victory over the eternal one-way love that he had offered the seas, the lands, the people, and that had never found a response. He would swim and be nude, he would learn to caress the waves, he would finally convince the sea that it had to accept him and love him.

Later, playing children would find the abandoned car by the beach, a pretty addition to sand castles and sun, but never would they find Don Juan who wanted to provide no proof: he had been a mistake by Wolfgang Mozart, a legend, a solid dream of Europe's last breaths of life.

Translator's Note

I begged off when Ariadne's Donald Daviau asked me if I wanted to append a note to my revision of the translation of *Plague in Siena*, this brilliant and profound conceit of the personae of the notorious Don Juan as a poetic discourse on love and death, fatigue and frenzy, the wisdom of youth, stupidity of old age, self-love and hatred, on the faith in eroticism as an escape from estrangement and self-enclosure, this wonderful chatterbox of a book among all the other wonderful things it is. Begged off, first, chiefly because I did not think that I could add anything to Joseph Strelka's foreword to the German paperback edition.

The second reason for my standing back was that I could not imagine that any comment of mine on what had seemed to me, on first enthusiastic encounter, the novel's fairly unselfconscious use of the style of the German Classical-Romantic tradition as the poets have made it a versatile medium during the past several centuries—which, initially, I did consider addressing—would add anything to what literary scholars, so I presume, MUST have said meanwhile on that subject. For, as compared to other contemporary Austrian writers who have made Herculean efforts to regain the classical tradition, Skwara seems to have been born into it, or, as I just said, so it seemed before I set out on the nitty-gritty of my work.

Except then, as I proceeded to respond with ever greater delight to Skwara's abilities, the myopic attention that a translator brings to his task alerted me to the possibility that I was in the hands of a jongleur, a Don Juan of words and styles, not just of limbs.

What can elicit those suspicions, most obviously, are those expressionistic modes that Skwara employs during Don Juan's encounter with Vincent van Gogh. In mind I have the two men stuttering, flailing around in pre-verbally awkward modes of expression. The exchange between Don Juan and Van Gogh is particularly archaic if we emphasize the "communion" aspect of the word communication. The attempt of fully grown men to babble the unutterable in the language of babes, who have no control yet of their voice boxes, that attempt invariably points to an emotional wish to articulate at the level of the near-symbiotic as is possible only between mother and child and from which stage, subsequently, we are excluded with the exception of the kind of controlled mutual regression that is possible between analyst and analysand in the psychoanalytic situation. And in poetry. What a lot of stuttering goes on there in those two arenas. Yet the straining expressionistic modes, too perhaps, have merely become part of the permanent reservoir of the German language; you can avail yourself of them, meanwhile, as the need arises, perhaps.

Delving more deeply, back-tracking into the available range of Skwara's styles, I was struck by his amazingly efficient use of poetic means for efficient elegant narrative purposes. The reader may wish to re-read the novel's opening and the immediately following Lake Compounce section, to be reminded of the richness embedded in so few paragraphs; within that anything but flowery style might want to focus on the use of colors to express moods—perhaps this is the living legacy of Georg Trakl, of a Trakl who has met Van Gogh; and who loves Rilke, and who can play arpeggios like Chopin. But the talent it takes to be profoundly influenced,—a talent far beyond mimicry or imitation "in the style of"—obviates any talk about influences except at the level of deepest yearning. Affinities of sensibilities. A multi-affinitied author then! with an affinity for the Pantheon.

To return once more, among the many times it would be possible to do so to my theme of Skwara as a possible virtuoso of language: in the book's ultimate chapter he avails himself, unless I am very much mistaken, of a possibly "sacrilegious" use of Stifterian idyllic means to portray Don Juan's expedition into the mountains: the ascent with the two youngsters, his last, though not totally consummated, "meal," the sight of the embalmed saint, etc. That is sacrilegious, if not perverse, not only from Church perspective, but also of the enshrinement of Adalbert Stifter, a classic Austrian writer, whom it is still very worthwhile to read for his poetic narrative modes, and whose idyllicism—

or the cover that Austrians take under his only superficial idyll—is given a nicely scandalous bow here.

Obvious features that I then noticed and nonetheless decide to point out also include what I shall call—Skwara hates irony—his wit, with which he feathers but not tars a figure who at times seems as insufferable as an iridescent humming bird: for example on the morning that Don Juan puts himself into a "literary mood" with wife and child still asleep. Yes, Don Juan suddenly has wife and child. It seems the woman in his last affair, which also came out of the blue, became pregnant, or so we presume—the cuts, or the lack of transitions, from section to section introduce some fine mysteries into a book that scarcely wants to be read in the mode of ordinary realism. The rules of Poetic Realism apply here. Yet here it is, the proposition: the aging Juan as father AND dandy, an impossibly amusing sequence that. As is his drive through Italy with the mother to be. We assume it is the same woman, but can't be sure.

There is much we would like to know about our tantalizing Don Juan after we have completed the book. There are those hundreds of years between his surviving the plague, his reappearance in French eighteenth century salons. Where did his spirit bide? In a village in Provence? Among the Transylvanians? How is it that he did not make the acquaintance of Baudelaire with all the other affinities he encounters? Are they too many to enumerate. We would like to read what he has in his suitcase. Is that his erotic past, of which he divulges so little, of this grand and endless Quixotic quest for true love across all those bodies that ultimately repel him, of which he bounces off for reasons of which he has no comprehension? Don Juan who calls himself a ghost may really be a neo-platonic spirit, a lost soul desperately searching to become embodied, yet restlessly he spits out what he has just devoured. Caught in that conflict of the oral triad, at the end he dissolves into that triad's third component, eternal sleep—the longed for watery death which is intimated, if that is the word for this persiflage of Thomas Mann's famous novella, early as the book's first page.

However, a psychoanalytically trained translator as I am—and the art of psychoanalysis too is nothing if not also the art of translating—could not help but bring to bear also this second kind of myopia on certain features of this particular Don Juan; who of course does not wish to be considered a case, or at least a very superior case, and who after all is a fiction. At least the invented 800-year-old Don Juan, in a basically double-track book, is a fiction and the other Don Juan, who travels on a younger track, aspires to emulate him while imagining, with the wisdom of the young, growing as old as his inspiring model. As young men would like to be Don Juans, as young women fancy themselves *femmes fatales*, although few possess the imaginations of such a two-fold Don Juan as the one of *Plague in Siena*. And so the question becomes whether and if the twin tracks on which they travel will or will not entwine, or do they only from the vantage of the vanishing point of infinity?

The matters which struck me from an analytic perspective however have little to do with anything of the erotic. The eroticism, which at any event is meant to lie chiefly in Don Juan's past, at least so he keeps saying, a past that he carries with him in a suitcase in his left hand, that eroticism simply is. Psychoanalysis has no need to explain eroticism, biologists do better at that.

Among a number of matters that the psychoanalytically oriented cannot help but notice, however, are Don Juan's inhibitions, who after all is no mere philanderer, as which of course he met his match many times over during the still remembered recent decades of polymorphous perversity, if only in the United States. For despite his libidinal staying powers over these centuries, the Don shies back, for fear of their possibly dirty underwear, from the pretty girls who stick like flies to a nightclub bar. A closet Don Juan possibly, or one that slips in and out, this younger of the two Don Juans, whose qualities become so tantalizingly mingled. Shy, chaste, a Don Juan who wants to stay pure as the driven snow! Guiltlessly guilty, with the innocence of the child that has just licked its first ice cream cone, this Don maintains his conviction that heaven resides in eroticism, an eroticism that ought to have the intelligence of a Chopin. Old as Don Juan is, there is about him that eternal quality of the next girl or boy being "the one!"

Yet for a Don Juan story the book contains few

erotic figures, narcissistically bisexual and eternally in love with youth as his inclination is, and perhaps to a somewhat greater extent than mankind as a whole. But I find it odd that over the centuries none of the 1000 plus creatures whom he attests to having seduced have left an imprint on him. I find it a little odd sometimes, that with those 800 years on his pelt, and aristocratic heritage, he is so lacking in self-assurance as to need to protest his superiority so much. (One might also note how very knowing, for a young writer's book, *Plague in Siena* is in matters concerning aging; though there will always, also, be John Updike's *The Poorhouse Fair.*)

Still, Don Juan mourns for two women who yet could not be more different from each other. One is the girl from Lake Compounce who looks to be the pure love that got away, and adoration of which purity the Don is perhaps incapable of except for brief spells—a youthful purity which he feels is only earned by the experience of old age, possible once he has passed through the purgatory of the plague.

That quality of being the girl who got away, if no other, is shared by Ms. Compounce's opposite, the pubescent, cruel Salome whom Maria Obolensky and Don Juan contemplate on the opera stage during Maria's miraculous but, qualitatively, necessary reappearance from the dead, as though chaste spiritual love, agape, and rutting love, as usual, are as incompatible as oil and water, endlessly conflicting. It is of course quite marvelous to have Salome's not necrophiliac's kiss of Jochanaan's cooling dead lips juxtaposed, within such few pages, to Don Juan's own skeletal kiss of Maria's virgin hand—sometimes it becomes difficult to tell how many parts of incidents such as these are perversity, humorous ghoulishness and/or felt longing.

Further, we may idly speculate why Don Juan is institutionalized for a time—erotomania would be a misdiagnosis I think; for erotomania might only be a screen to cover his anxieties. Anxiety too can be a screen for other, worse, things. As I said, we can speculate. But perhaps the author just put Don Juan in the *maison de santé* so he would be in the proper mood for his encounter with yet another alter ego, Van Gogh! Or it made for a good scene in this also very operatic book. Or all or none of these things or any combination thereof.

But what bowled me over, at the rate of a couple of my mental pins per page, what really wrenched my mind around inside my head, are certain turns of phrase, Skwara's turn of mind that comes out of a blue that I had not imagined existed. Far out. From the leftest left field, an American wants to exclaim. Extra-ordinary, and not just stylistically: ". . . even though I suffered only a small share of my lust in that part of Europe . . ." "When the muteness of encounters remained like blue smoke on the road . . ." "Because less and less becomes sayable, because hardly a word can survive, speech grows poorer and yet the wealth of our silences sees no surfeit". . . ."Because we cannot weep, because we cannot love, we want to speak and find the words that will justify what makes us fall silent.". . ."The girl had invited guests to the summer festival who knew the extent of mourning in which the gardens lie embedded. The girl had not planned the summer festival; rather she had raised it as others raise children, with all possible care, with all possible love.". . . "This locking [of the suitcase] became the most important item of his departure; his life would stand or fall with the closed suitcase lock. For it only made sense to have a suitcase if you were never to open it again. Possessing a suitcase is justified only if its contents are familiar to the owner; otherwise the case will turn into a nightmare" . . . "A unit of disillusionment had been added here, but how does one measure this unit? In questioning, in silence, in burned-out candles?". . ."How ridiculously weak the murdered are."—But enough. And why analyze it? Though it can be done. The readers, unless they be those who read postscripts first, will have been unsettled out of their accustomed ruts by the time they reach this page.

Michael Roloff

About the Author:

Austrian poet, novelist and essayist Erich Wolfgang Skwara was born in 1948 in Salzburg. As a journalist, critic, interpreter and free-lance author, he has traveled worldwide and regularly contributes to a number of leading German and Austrian newspapers and magazines. The first of his five collections of poetry was published in 1971; the most recent, entitled *Den Abschied proben* (To Rehearse Farewell), is presently being translated for publication in English. His novels to date are *Pest in Siena*, presented here as the second of Skwara's novels in English, *Schwarze Segelschiffe*, *Bankrottidylle* (published in translation as *The Cool Million* by Ariadne Press in 1990), *Eis auf der Brücke*, and in 1992, *Tristan Island*. In addition, E.W. Skwara has published a collection of short stories, *Der Totenengel*, and the biography *Hans Sahl: Leben und Werk*. He holds a doctorate in German and French literatures and divides his time between Salzburg, Paris, and San Diego, California, where he is Professor of Humanities and Comparative Literature. Erich Wolfgang Skwara is a member of the Austrian and French Centers of the International P.E.N. Club.

ARIADNE PRESS

Studies in Austrian Literature, Culture and Thought

Major Figures of Modern Austrian Literature
Edited and Introduced by Donald G. Daviau

Major Figures of Turn-of-the-Century Austrian Literature
Edited and Introduced by Donald G. Daviau

Austrian Writers and the Anschluss: Understanding the Past—Overcoming the Past
Edited and Introduced by Donald G. Daviau

Introducing Austria A Short History
By Lonnie Johnson

Coexistent Contradictions Joseph Roth in Retrospect
Edited by Helen Chambers

The Verbal and Visual Art of Alfred Kubin
By Phillip H. Rhein

Kafka and Language In the Stream of Thoughts and Life
By G. von Natzmer Cooper

Robert Musil and the Tradition of the German Novelle
By Kathleen O'Connor

Blind Reflections: Gender in Elias Canetti's Die Blendung
By Kristie A. Foell

Conversations with Peter Rosei
By Wilhelm Schwarz

Austria in the Thirties Culture and Politics
Edited by Kenneth Segar and John Warren

Stefan Zweig: An International Bibliography
By Randolph J. Klawiter

Austrian Foreign Policy Yearbook
Report of the Austrian Federal Ministry for Foreign Affairs for the Year 1990

Quietude and Quest Protagonists and Antagonists in the Theater, on and off Stage As Seen Through the Eyes of Leon Askin
Leon Askin and C. Melvin Davidson

"What People Call Pessimism": Sigmund Freud, Arthur Schnitzler and Nineteenth-Century Controversy at the University of Vienna Medical School
By Mark Luprecht

Arthur Schnitzler and Politics
By Adrian Clive Roberts

Structures of Disintegration Narrative Strategies in Elias Canetti's Die Blendung
By David Darby

Of Reason and Love The Life and Work of Marie von Ebner-Eschenbach
By Carl Steiner

Franz Kafka: A Writers Life
By Joachim Unseld

Translations:

The Bengal Tiger
By Jeannie Ebner
Translation and Afterword
by Lowell A. Bangerter

Three Flute Notes
By Jeannie Ebner
Translation and Afterword
by Lowell A. Bangerter

Farewell to Love and Other Misunderstandings
By Herbert Eisenreich
Translation and Afterword
by Renate Latimer

The Sphere of Glass
By Marianne Gruber
Translation and Afterword
by Alexandra Strelka
Preface by Joseph P. Strelka

A Man Too White
By György Sebestén
Translation and Afterword
by Michael Mitchell

The Green Face
By Gustav Meyrink
Translated by Michael Mitchell

The Ariadne Book of Austrian Fantasy
The Meyrink Years 1890-1930
Edited and translated
by Michael Mitchell

Walpurgisnacht
By Gustav Meyrink
Translated by Michael Mitchell

On the Wrong Track
By Milo Dor
Translated by Jerry Glenn
and Jennifer Kelley

Night Train
By Friederike Mayröcker
Translation and Afterword
by Beth Bjorklund

Memories With Trees
By Ilse Tielsch
Translation and Afterword
by David Scrase

Return to the Center
By Otto von Habsburg
Translated by Carvel de Bussy

View from a Distance
By Lore Lizbeth Waller

Five Plays
By Gerald Szyszkowitz
Translated by Todd Hanlin, Heidi Hutchinson and Joseph McVeigh

Anthology of Contemporary Austrian Folk Plays
By Veza Canetti, Peter Preses & Ulrich Becher, Felix Mitterer, Gerald Szyszkowitz, Peter Turrini
Translation and Afterword
by Richard Dixon

The Condemned Judge
By Janko Ferk
Translation and Afterword
by Lowell A. Bangerter

Thomas Bernhard and His Grandfather: "Our Grandfathers Are Our Teachers."
By Caroline Markolin
Translated by Petra Hartweg

The Convent School
By Barbara Frischmuth
Translated by
Gerald Chapple and James B. Lawson

The Calm Ocean
By Gerhard Roth
Translated by Helga Schreckenberger
and Jacqueline Vansant

Remembering Gardens
by Kurt Klinger
Translated by Harvey I. Dunkle